SHORTCUT 6
376 POWER QUOTES

by LINKED IN AND TOWN HALL ACHIEVER OF THE YEAR
EY NOMINEE ENTREPRENEUR OF THE YEAR
GRAND HOMAGE LYS DIVERSITY
WORLD TOP100 DOCTORS

Dr BAK NGUYEN, DMD

TO ALL THOSE LOOKING TO WALK THIS IS THE KEY TO ACCESS THEIR WEAPON AND TOOLS GOD INTENDED FOR YOU.

by Dr BAK NGUYEN

Copyright © 2021 Dr. BAK NGUYEN

All rights reserved.

ISBN: 978-1-989536-80-3

Published by: Dr. BAK PUBLISHING COMPANY
Dr.BAK 0098

DISCLAIMER

« The general information, opinions and advice contained in this medium and/or the books, audiobooks, podcasts and publications on Dr. Bak Nguyen's (legal name Dr. Ba Khoa Nguyen) website or social media (hereinafter the "Opinions") present general information on various topics. The Opinions are intended for informational purposes only.

No information contained in the Opinions is a substitute for an expert, consultation, advice, diagnosis or professional treatment. No information contained in the Opinions is a substitute for professional advice and should not be construed as consultation or advice.

Nothing in the Opinions should be construed as professional advice related to the practice of dentistry, medical advice or any other form of advice, including legal or financial advice, professional opinion, care or diagnosis, but strictly as general information. All information from the Opinions is for informational purposes only.

Any user who disagrees with the terms of this Disclaimer should immediately cease using or referring to the Opinions. Any action by the user in connection with the information contained in the Opinions is solely at the user's discretion.

The general information contained in the Opinions is provided "as is" and without warranty of any kind, either expressed or implied. Dr. Bak Nguyen (legal name Dr. Ba Khoa Nguyen) makes every effort to ensure that the information is complete and accurate. However, there is no guarantee that the general information contained in the Opinions is always available, truthful, complete, up-to-date or relevant.

The Opinions expressed by Dr. Bak Nguyen (legal name Dr. Ba Khoa Nguyen) are personal and expressed in his own name and do not reflect the opinions of his companies, partners and other affiliates.

Dr. Bak Nguyen (legal name Dr. Ba Khoa Nguyen) also disclaims any responsibility for the content of any hyperlinks included in the Opinions.

Always seek the advice of your expert advisors, physicians or other qualified professionals with any questions you may have regarding your condition. Never disregard professional advice or delay in seeking it because of something you have read, seen or heard in the Opinions. »

ABOUT THE AUTHOR

From Canada, **Dr. BAK NGUYEN**, Nominee Ernst and Young Entrepreneur of the year, Grand Homage Lys DIVERSITY, LinkedIn & TownHall Achiever of the year and TOP 100 Doctors 2021. Dr Bak is a cosmetic dentist, CEO and founder of Mdex & Co. His company is revolutionizing the dental field. Speaker and motivator, he wrote 72 books over 36 months accumulating many world records (to be officialized). His books are covering:

- **ENTREPRENEURSHIP**
- **LEADERSHIP**
- **QUEST OF IDENTITY**
- **DENTISTRY AND MEDICINE**
- **PARENTING**
- **CHILDREN'S BOOKS**
- **PHILOSOPHY**

In 2003, he founded Mdex, a dental company upon which in 2018, he launched the most ambitious private endeavour to reform the dental industry, Canada wide. Philosopher, he has close to his heart the quest of happiness of the people surrounding him, patients and colleagues alike. In 2020, he launched an International collaborative initiative named **THE ALPHAS** to share knowledge and for Entrepreneurs and Doctors to thrive through the Greatest Pandemic and Economic depression of our time.

In 2016, he co-found with Tranie Vo, Emotive World Incorporated, a tech research company to use technology to empower happiness and sharing. U.A.X. the ultimate audio experience is the landmark project on which the team is advancing, utilizing the technics of the movie industry and the advancement in ARTIFICIAL INTELLIGENCE to save the book industry and to upgrade the continuing education space.

These projects have allowed Dr Nguyen to attract interests from the international and diplomatic community and he is now the centre of a global discussion in the wellbeing and the future of the health profession. It is in that matter that he shares his thoughts and encourages the health community to share their own stories.

> "It's not worth it go through it alone! Together, we stand, alone, we fall."

Motivational speaker and serial entrepreneur, philosopher and author, from his own words, Dr Nguyen describes himself as a dentist by circumstances, an entrepreneur by nature and a communicator by passion.

He also holds recognitions from the Canadian Parliament and the Canadian Senate.

SHORTCUT 6
376 POWER QUOTES

by Dr BAK NGUYEN

INTRODUCTION
BY Dr BAK NGUYEN

PART 1
POWER
Dr. BAK NGUYEN

PART 2
184 POWER QUOTES
Dr. BAK NGUYEN

PART 3
LIFE
Dr. BAK NGUYEN

PART 4
73 LIFE QUOTES
Dr. BAK NGUYEN

PART 5
TIME
Dr. BAK NGUYEN

PART 6
67 TIME QUOTES
Dr. BAK NGUYEN

PART 7
ABUNDANCE
Dr. BAK NGUYEN

PART 8
52 ABUNDANCE QUOTES
Dr. BAK NGUYEN

PART 9
THE POWER OF QUOTES
Dr. BAK NGUYEN

PART 10
77 FAMOUS QUOTES
Dr. BAK NGUYEN

CONCLUSION
BY Dr BAK NGUYEN

ANNEX
GLOSSARY OF Dr. BAK's LIBRARY
Dr. BAK NGUYEN

INTRODUCTION
by Dr. BAK NGUYEN

INTRODUCTION

Time flies so quickly. I just finished the publishing of my latest book, **TIMING, TIME MANAGEMENT ON STEROIDS**. It is already available on Apple Books and Amazon Kindle. I am waiting for its imminent release as COMBO paperback/audiobook on Amazon, later today.

TIMING, TIME MANAGEMENT ON STEROIDS will be book #74 to replace **COVIDCONOMICS** that will arrive later, much later. As I was writing the conclusion, my odds were 5 days per book (with 4 books left to write).

I must say how pleasant it was to break the routine and to write on a completely different matter… and to produce an audiobook too! The last audiobook that I produced was months ago, before the **SHORTCUT franchise**.

The end of the writing of **TIMING** also coincided with my clinical duty, 2 full days in clinic. Today, it is Saturday. As I am writing this introduction, my odds are down to 4.25 days per book for the next 4 books left to write before August 31st.

I was a doctor for 2 days and my odds went down from 5 to 4.25 days. That's 0.75 days that I just lost per book! In others terms, I just lost 18 hours of writing time per book.

That's depressing but that's also ok. I have the same exact feeling as I am driving long distances following the GPS.

I am cutting the minutes before arrival and as soon as we stop for gas or for a break, we screw up our numbers royally. Well, I was not taking a break, I was resuming my duty as a doctor. I also had a few executive meetings to lead my company, **Mdex & Co.** for its soon to open expansion and international negotiations. More than once, you read about my duty piling up as a doctor, a CEO, and a world record author.

Well, this time, I wanted to share with you the feeling and the numbers. I haven't slowed down and yet, I lost 18 hours per book! God knows that I needed these 18 hours to have a chance to score the next world record of writing 100 books within 4 years!

But here I am, this morning, ready to start yet, another journey. The prep work was done and finished yesterday before hitting bed, as the publishing of **TIMING** was submitted to Amazon. To receive the confirmation that the KINDLE version was released this morning was a great boost in confidence.

And this is the energy with which I am pushing forward in the 6th journey of **SHORTCUT**. **SHORTCUT**, what a misleading title, not to you, because it is real that shortcut will ease your way and speed up your evolution and personal growth. It is misleading to me! The **SHORTCUT series** has taken everything out of me. It was and still is very demanding and the biggest and most challenging endeavour I have tackled as an author.

I guess that I have to work as hard so once the work is done, yours will be easier. Nothing is free, ever. That said, **SHORTCUT** is also the most clarified map that I discovered to personal growth and for its leverage. So enjoy the ride, yours will be easier than mine was, not just the experience but also the writing!

> "Leverage, I love that word. It is not enough to grow, one still has to find use of ones' powers."
> Dr. Bak Nguyen

That's quote #2501. And here comes the 6th volume of **SHORTCUT, POWER**! Yes, you are now ready. Knowing that growth happens at the giving end, knowing that to grow and rise with lesser resistance, you need to serve others, you are now ready to find more and more powers.

I told you about the deepest fear that I have, was to show up in front of God and not present with as many talents as he expects. In a nightmare that I still remember sharply each of its detail, I was giving back the 3 talents that I received and presenting 3 more as profit. Well, I lost all of myself as I heard: "What are you talking about, I gave you 10!" And this is how I came up with one of my signature quote:

> "My deepest fear is to show up before God and not have enough to show for."
> Dr. Bak Nguyen

Well, talents are powers that I found travelling my journeys, going from win to win. Each win is building up my **Confidence, experience, boldness**, and **wisdom**.

Yes, I am **bolder** since I know what I am and what I am not. At the same time, I am also wiser because I know that everything that is found and given can also be taken away and lost forever. And there is no worst feeling than to feel the empowerment once, only to never be felt again.

As I am travelling my journey to find my purpose and to serve, I am giving without holding back to just cross the finished line. That was at the beginning of my awakening. Today, I've learnt to go all-in but also, not to over-extend myself since this won't be my last journey.

And that's the **wisdom** that I gained travelling Life and Growth, I learnt to jump from win to win, to not swallow more than I can take. I know that I will eat it all, only, I need to survive and enjoy that bite and growth too!

So wisdom allowed me to go even further, faster because I am not burning myself at each footstep any more. That's the how. The where, well, that one has increased exponentially in boldness and horizon!

And this is what you will be learning travelling this journey with me, how and where to find and to harness your powers. Power you are and power you have.

"To touch power, stay in movement, otherwise, you will be burning yourself standing still holding power."
Dr. Bak Nguyen

That's quote #2502. Read that one again. For your own sake, read it once more! You cannot hold power and to stand still, this is suicide, torture if you survive it, and even worst, the **SCARS OF POWER** will corrupt your code forever!

So more than finding power, I will also prepare you to yield it, to leverage it so you are the master and not the tool. Because power is a tool, a great one, but it can also be a slave master if you were not prepared.

And guess what, there are as many powers as there are stars in the sky. So as many opportunities and slave masters looking to enslave you! Amongst the **RISING volumes**, this one is the darkest one. One that will seduce you with promises and one that will entice you with, maybe, more than you bargained for.

This is **Shortcut volume 6, POWER**. Welcome to the Alphas.

Hammering air three times over and it will become steel.

Dr. BAK NGUYEN

PART 1
"POWER"
by Dr. BAK NGUYEN

Power is such a double edges sword. Power is great and can be enticing. Power will also corrupt and take over each and everyone of us if we do not yield it properly nor have let it go when we should have.

I know, you are confused. What power are we talking about? Is it power with a capital P, meaning being in command, or is it the powers within each of us? Well, power is power.

Like the infamous phrase, with great power comes great responsibilities, power is only useful as one is faced with a task, a challenge. Once that challenge is completed, if the one holding power does not put it back to use as quickly as possible, power will turn its strength against the **bearer** and the corruption starts. It has been the same story since the beginning of age.

Are you ready to find and to yield your powers? Are you ready to do great with these borrowed powers? Power is not a right nor a status but a tool. More than once, I referred to being in **synergy** with the Universe, yielding power will elevate your energy to do so. And since the Universe is flowing and in constant movement, so will you have to be too.

You read about my journeys and how I discovered my powers, those gave me back my wings. You also know about my **fear of God**, showing up short of talents at **judgment day**. Well, the real story is more complex than that.

> "Growth happens at the giving end."
> Dr. Bak Nguyen

That is something that we know by now. Earlier in my journey, I sensed that truth with another quote: "Sharing is the way to grow." Well, this is because power is never given, it is found. A talent to write, the gift of creativity, the ease to dance, the voice of music, we each have our share of the divine.

We all know that each talent will push us forward for more. That journey is the beginning of our rise. As we are reaching the **checkpoints** and putting our talents to good use, Confidence will grow and we will be yielding that talent, not just discovering its power. From there, what we do is up to us, it is part of our legend.

Will you inspire the world, heal the world our stop a war, it all comes down to your talents (powers) and how you choose to exercise them. Well, I did my best with the talents that God gave me. I pushed and I pushed, looking for the boundaries, the limits. This is how I became an overachiever.

To minimize resistance and useless fighting, I learnt to use my talents while helping others. I am not saying that there is no friction, but it is definitively less as the people you help are putting their trust in you. With trust, Confidence grew. And so is jealousy… be warned.

> "With more Confidence, I kept my heart and mind open to do more, to learn more."
> **Dr. Bak Nguyen**

That's quote #2503. I do first and then, I learn, contrary to common wisdom. I am not talking about education and Conformity here, I am talking about the journey and the way to learn. I told you time and time again that I am jumping from win to win.

Well, in between, the lessons learnt are mostly not to stop on a win, no matter how big or how small. And the biggest lessons on the way are these liabilities, these defeats I hit on the way. If that is not the final entry in my journey, that's the next challenge.

> "Leverage your liabilities and you will always
> be moving forward."
> Dr. Bak Nguyen

Some, I was smart and strong enough to leverage into my next wins. Some others, I still carry around, waiting to be ready to tackle one day. The goal is to let go of the wins to keep moving as lightweight as possible. The problems are the liabilities and defeats, those are following me around, even closer than my own shadow. In time, I will clean them too.

But let's go back a minute. What do you think happens when you turn a liability into a challenge? Well, you have to swallow your pride, learn and change your approach, art, and science to do more, to do better. That's learning, at its purest! That's why to learn, one has to do first!

Some I will win and some I will lose, again. Maybe I was not ready, maybe it was not the right time yet. I pick myself up and before doubt has the time to settle in, I will jump to my next challenge, perhaps, a smaller one, just to feed my momentum and morale. Eventually, I will face that same challenge again and will come out on top, eventually.

The day that I come out on top of such challenge, I will have outgrown myself, I will have turned a liability into a positive experience. In other words, I have found a new power and boosted my Confidence.

The feeling of satisfaction is unique and hard to describe, I am in symbiosis, even in synergy with the Universe as it happens. But shortly after, each time, I realize that I just found a new power, one that I will have to deliver on too!

And that is my blessing. Using the wrong mindset and wording, some will say that it is my curse. The facts are the same, only the perception is different. Is that just a matter of words? Unfortunately not. It will define our future and evolution.

"The choice of wording is setting the themes of our lives."
Dr. Bak Nguyen

That's quote #2504. As I am seeing a blessing, I am grateful and will deliver. Doing so, I am back on a new journey, with no time for neither doubt nor boredom. More importantly, I am not a victim of power since I am staying in movement.

The powers that are useful for my next journey, I keep with me. Those that are not, well, I clean them with love and respect and leave them behind for someone else to find. I painted that picture very vividly in **MINDSET ARMORY**, my 50th book.

Back then, all I knew was that I wanted to keep moving lightweight. Now, I realized that the wisdom was more profound, it was to not be burned alive by these same forces that we once yielded.

> "Power is not a status nor it is permanent.
> Power is always growing, always looking for more."
> **Dr. Bak Nguyen**

That's quote #2505. As it is growing, Power needs to keep walking the challenge and the journeys. In fact, we do not yield power, we never did. It is just that power will follow our lead for as long as we are feeding it with more wins. We might grow old, sick and tire, power does not.

And this is how I found my powers, walking from one journey to the next. I discovered powers, yielded them, and grew at each turn. Then, my fear of God pushed me forward. I am serving God, not the powers that I found. So, more than once, in the middle of a honeymoon, I kiss these powers goodbye, until we meet again.

This is how I managed to do more within the last 4 years than in my first 40.

> "I am a generous soul with everyone.
> Why be cheat with myself?"
> **Dr. Bak Nguyen**

That's quote #2506. That and the fear of God protected me from getting drunk by power and falling victim to it. About cleaning my tools and powers and leaving them behind for someone to find, what do you think that I am doing here, sharing with you?

You don't have to thank me, polishing the powers before leaving them behind gives me closure and allows me the time for farewells. Again, I am growing as much as when I was yielding them!

Thanks to that mentality and the habits coming with it, I became a champion of power. Powers love me. And by power, I am not talking about management, but the forces of the Universe. More than once, I have teamed up again with powers that I once departed. The reunion was legendary. Writing is one of these stories.

Very briefly, I was back in college and growing bored with my studies when I first discovered the power of writing. I wrote a few short stories and did not think much of them. A few years later, that brought me to direct an independent movie when I was in dental school.

Around the same time, I also had a broken heart. Writing short stories was my way back to sanity. I loved that passage but then, Life took over and I became a dentist. For almost 20 years, I left that power in my past… until it presents itself at the dawn of my rise as Dr. Bak.

Then, our union became legendary, writing world records after world records. I don't even have the time to stop to submit my world record for officialization. That will come, eventually. I am yielding that power of communication to new heights, my mission is to keep moving and to share, with you!

The last 4 years, I discovered so many powers as I am accelerating my acceleration. Writing has become second nature, inspiring people and leadership were from the new powers that joined the band. Creativity, music are also companions that I have the privilege to share energy with.

From one journey to the next, I will go with some and will say goodbye to others. But since we are energy and kinetic, we will find each other again, at the next rest areas on one of these journeys.

> "The crossroads are as abundant as the stars but somehow, we all meet there, again and again."
> **Dr. Bak Nguyen**

That's quote #2507. Don't fool yourself, thinking that you can possess power. You do not choose it, it chooses you. That's your first lesson looking for power.

To be successful, don't seek Power
It will find you.
Be available, open, and ready.
And Power will come knocking.

Be humble and maybe, Power will stay.

To yield Power, be kind and generous.
To attract Power, be independent and grateful.
To become Power, keep pushing.

This is **Shortcut volume 6, POWER**. Welcome to the Alphas.

Hammering air three times over
and it will become steel.

Dr. BAK NGUYEN

PART 2
"184 POWER QUOTES"
by Dr. BAK NGUYEN

1557
FROM SYMPHONY OF SKILLS
"The greatness is in the number of possible connections!"
Dr. Bak Nguyen

1558
FROM SYMPHONY OF SKILLS
"The power of positive energy grows exponentially as shared."
Dr. Bak Nguyen

1559
FROM SYMPHONY OF SKILLS
"You have to make your own truth."
Dr. Bak Nguyen

1560
FROM LEADERSHIP, PANDORA'S BOX
"Hope is the Will within every single heart."
Dr. Bak Nguyen

1561
FROM LEADERSHIP, PANDORA'S BOX
"That's the power of Hope; it starts small and grows into a storm."
Dr. Bak Nguyen

1562
FROM LEADERSHIP, PANDORA'S BOX
"History is masterpieced with the palette of Greed. Good and bad, but always great!"
Dr. Bak Nguyen

1563
FROM LEADERSHIP, PANDORA'S BOX
"Failing to understand the dynamics of power between the heart and the mind will have catastrophic consequences."
Dr. Bak Nguyen

1564
FROM LEADERSHIP, PANDORA'S BOX
" Don't stand in the way of a loyal heart because there is no victory possible."
Dr. Bak Nguyen

1565
FROM LEADERSHIP, PANDORA'S BOX
"The 10% will ease the day because 100% is leading the way."
Dr. Bak Nguyen

1566
FROM LEADERSHIP, PANDORA'S BOX
"100% belief, 100% will, 10% knowledge, and 110% evolution."
Dr. Bak Nguyen

1567
FROM LEADERSHIP, PANDORA'S BOX
"To create is a privilege, a privilege to reorganize the Universe and to have access to its fabric."
Dr. Bak Nguyen

1568
FROM LEADERSHIP, PANDORA'S BOX
"The vitality of creativity is an enhanced formula to Happiness and Greatness."
Dr. Bak Nguyen

1569
FROM LEADERSHIP, PANDORA'S BOX
"Free and Will. We have. We are."
Dr. Bak Nguyen

1570
FROM LEADERSHIP, PANDORA'S BOX
"The only force without a shadow is our Will."
Dr. Bak Nguyen

1571
FROM LEADERSHIP, PANDORA'S BOX
"The strength of your Will will dictate the world we are living in."

Dr. Bak Nguyen

1572
FROM LEADERSHIP, PANDORA'S BOX
"As One is not whole, one is not unity."

Dr. Bak Nguyen

1573
FROM LEADERSHIP, PANDORA'S BOX
"To divide is not divine. To subtract is not natural."

Dr. Bak Nguyen

1574
FROM IDENTITY, ANTHOLOGY OF QUESTS
"Momentum is not something that goes away in an instant. So master the essence of spend to capitalize on it. Otherwise, it will pass you by and even roll over your body."

Dr. Bak Nguyen

1575
FROM IDENTITY, ANTHOLOGY OF QUESTS
"True power is the awareness of one's self."

Dr. Bak Nguyen

1576
FROM IDENTITY, ANTHOLOGY OF QUESTS
"Seduction is our way to unify yourself and taste synergy!"
Dr. Bak Nguyen

1577
FROM IDENTITY, ANTHOLOGY OF QUESTS
"To foresee the future, one must master the chords of life."
Dr. Bak Nguyen

1578
FROM IDENTITY, ANTHOLOGY OF QUESTS
"Balance is not the state of Nirvana, just what is, while we are still wondering where to go."
Dr. Bak Nguyen

1579
FROM PROFESSION HEALTH
"Compounding taught me patience and resilience."
Dr. Bak Nguyen

1580
FROM PROFESSION HEALTH
"Power was the consequence, not the goal."
Dr. Bak Nguyen

1581
FROM PROFESSION HEALTH
"Whatever we are thinking will be our tomorrow."
Dr. Bak Nguyen

1582
FROM INDUSTRIES' DISRUPTORS
"Momentum, that's the power behind the launch of any idea."
Dr. Bak Nguyen

1583
FROM INDUSTRIES' DISRUPTORS
"So I did, I became the guy who said yes!"
Dr. Bak Nguyen

1584
FROM INDUSTRIES' DISRUPTORS
"Before, the entrepreneur only has his will as power. As a disruptor, he now has a purpose greater than himself to empower his journey."
Dr. Bak Nguyen

1585
FROM INDUSTRIES' DISRUPTORS
"The lion will always outgrow its cage,
that's in its nature."
Dr. Bak Nguyen

1586
FROM INDUSTRIES' DISRUPTORS
"I advance in this life fearless because
the only fear I have is not from this world."
Dr. Bak Nguyen

1587
FROM INDUSTRIES' DISRUPTORS
"…to transform fear into hope,
the hope to be worthy."
Dr. Bak Nguyen

1588
FROM INDUSTRIES' DISRUPTORS
"Greed and Fear are two faces of the same coin."
Dr. Bak Nguyen

1589
FROM INDUSTRIES' DISRUPTORS
"To grow power, one has to free oneself
from his or her embodiment."
Dr. Bak Nguyen

1590
FROM INDUSTRIES' DISRUPTORS
"The quest for influence allowed me to free myself
from my own pride and to accept that
I was replaceable."
Dr. Bak Nguyen

1591
FROM INDUSTRIES' DISRUPTORS
"The quest for influence freed me
from my own embodiment."
Dr. Bak Nguyen

1592
FROM CHANGING THE WORLD FROM A DENTAL CHAIR
" I react to my own actions.
That's a way to embrace momentum."
Dr. Bak Nguyen

1593
FROM CHANGING THE WORLD FROM A DENTAL CHAIR
"Technology: learn to master it.
It is the modern ride of today's knights."
Dr. Bak Nguyen

1594
FROM CHANGING THE WORLD FROM A DENTAL CHAIR
"It's crazy what you can do
when you are empowered!"
Dr. Bak Nguyen

1595
FROM CHANGING THE WORLD FROM A DENTAL CHAIR
"Capitalize now on what's available
and feed your momentum."
Dr. Bak Nguyen

1596
FROM THE POWER BEHIND THE ALPHA
"What made the woman a power woman
is the leap of faith she took."
Dr. Bak Nguyen

1597
FROM THE POWER BEHIND THE ALPHA
" Power women are women refusing to bow down to what society has in mind for them. Not by revolting against men, but by loving their chosen ones."
Dr. Bak Nguyen

1598
FROM THE POWER BEHIND THE ALPHA
"Peace allows me to build with the strength of a tornado."
Dr. Bak Nguyen

1599
FROM MOMENTUM TRANSFER
" The EYE of my momentum is the depth of awareness of what I can achieve. "
Dr. Bak Nguyen

1600
FROM MOMENTUM TRANSFER
" Control is an dangerous illusion, especially when the Ego gets in the mix."
Dr. Bak Nguyen

1601
FROM MOMENTUM TRANSFER
"To stabilize a momentum, speed up!"
Dr. Bak Nguyen

1602
FROM MOMENTUM TRANSFER
" A momentum without resistance is named a flow. The flow of life."
Dr. Bak Nguyen

1603
FROM MOMENTUM TRANSFER
"In movement, feelings and thoughts tend to dim down. Sensations are king"
Dr. Bak Nguyen

1604
FROM MOMENTUM TRANSFER
"My EYE was found and I am now whole."
Dr. Bak Nguyen

1605
FROM MOMENTUM TRANSFER
"The danger of passion without self control is to be the storm destroying all of what you hold dear to your heart."
Dr. Bak Nguyen

1606
FROM MOMENTUM TRANSFER
"With the power of momentum in your hand, be wise, generous and kind."
Dr. Bak Nguyen

1607
FROM HYBRID
"Speed is my power. Momentum, my expression."
Dr. Bak Nguyen

1608
FROM HYBRID
"The diversity of the combinations of energies is the wonder and beauty if the universe."
Dr. Bak Nguyen

1609
FROM HYBRID
"Worth leads to more powers... real superpower."
Dr. Bak Nguyen

1610
FROM HYBRID
"Fun is the motor to my evolution. Not pain."
Dr. Bak Nguyen

1611
FROM HYBRID
"Knowing your chords and recognizing the pattern, to find the missing link is sometime much easier if you allow yourself to feel."
Dr. Bak Nguyen

1612
FROM HYBRID
"Nothing is more powerful than a true WILL."
Dr. Bak Nguyen

1613
FROM HYBRID
"My speed is not about how fast I move, but about how fast I adapt."
Dr. Bak Nguyen

1614
FROM HYBRID
"The greater the void, the bigger the attraction."
Dr. Bak Nguyen

1615
FROM LEVERAGE COMMUNICATION INTO SUCCESS
"Stronger the image, stronger the emotions"
Dr. Bak Nguyen

1616
FROM LEVERAGE COMMUNICATION INTO SUCCESS
"Emotions are powerful motivators.
Understand emotions and you will know the future."
Dr. Bak Nguyen

1617
FROM LEVERAGE COMMUNICATION INTO SUCCESS
"Empathy is a superpower."
Dr. Bak Nguyen

1618
FROM LEVERAGE COMMUNICATION INTO SUCCESS
"If you listen, they are dying to tell you everything about them, even if they are shy."
Dr. Bak Nguyen

1619
FROM LEVERAGE COMMUNICATION INTO SUCCESS
"Show people what they want to keep power. Show people what they don't expect to grow in power"
Dr. Bak Nguyen

1620
FROM LEVERAGE COMMUNICATION INTO SUCCESS
"If there is no leverage, there is no interest."
Dr. Bak Nguyen

1621
FROM FORCES OF NATURE
"Flexibility of the mind, it is the strongest ability."
Dr. Bak Nguyen

1622
FROM FORCES OF NATURE
"I walk and my skills clear the way. not walking the way that my skills can clean."
Dr. Bak Nguyen

1623
FROM FORCES OF NATURE
"Power is about usefulness, not demonstration."
Dr. Bak Nguyen

1624
FROM FORCES OF NATURE
"To develop my inner powers, I embraced laziness."
Dr. Bak Nguyen

1625
FROM THE BOOK OF LEGENDS, VOLUME 1
"If anything, I speed up to keep feeding my momentum."
Dr. Bak Nguyen

1626
FROM SELFMADE
"The sources of all my new achievements and powers are my flexibility and openness."
Dr. Bak Nguyen

1627
FROM SELFMADE
"Openness and Momentum, that how I build, and I started now!"
Dr. Bak Nguyen

1628
FROM SELFMADE
"Relationship is about feelings, not fact."
Dr. Bak Nguyen

1629
FROM SELFMADE
"Stay light, stay focus, stay open to be fluid."
Dr. Bak Nguyen

1630
FROM POWER, EMOTIONAL INTELLIGENCE
"Momentum is the counterweight to my emotional balance."
Dr. Bak Nguyen

1631
FROM POWER, EMOTIONAL INTELLIGENCE
"That's EMOTIONAL INTELLIGENCE, to learn to surf!"
Dr. Bak Nguyen

1632
FROM POWER, EMOTIONAL INTELLIGENCE
"The power is both from the outside and from within. To become powerful, one must synchronize both."
Dr. Bak Nguyen

1633
FROM POWER, EMOTIONAL INTELLIGENCE
"The first rule of emotional intelligence is sympathy."
Dr. Bak Nguyen

1634
FROM POWER, EMOTIONAL INTELLIGENCE
"Being a good listener is the easiest way to start to gather intelligence. But nothing is free in life…"
Dr. Bak Nguyen

1635
FROM POWER, EMOTIONAL INTELLIGENCE
"Reading people is a two-way street."
Dr. Bak Nguyen

1636
FROM POWER, EMOTIONAL INTELLIGENCE
"This book is not about understanding EMOTIONAL INTELLIGENCE, but about accessing its POWER."
Dr. Bak Nguyen

1637
FROM POWER, EMOTIONAL INTELLIGENCE
"Influence is to tell someone what will be and to have no expectation."
Dr. Bak Nguyen

1638
FROM BRANDING
"Momentum starts will one.
The power of the crowd starts with three."
Dr. Bak Nguyen

1639
FROM BRANDING
"Once I broke the sound barrier, stopping was simply not on the table anymore."
Dr. Bak Nguyen

1640
FROM HORIZON VOLUME ONE
"Without my imagination, I am a hero without superpower."
Dr. Bak Nguyen

1641
FROM HORIZON VOLUME ONE
"Live your life as a movie and your imagination will be your wings."
Dr. Bak Nguyen

1642
FROM THE POWER OF YES, VOLUME 1
"A free heart is the most powerful heart."

Dr. Bak Nguyen

1643
FROM HORIZON VOLUME TWO
"Do not touch my Momentum!"

Dr. Bak Nguyen

1644
FROM HORIZON VOLUME TWO
"Open and secure are two opposites, but once united, one can hold power beyond imagination."

Dr. Bak Nguyen

1645
FROM THE POWER OF YES VOLUME 3
"The keys are respect and openness. and what is openness but those three letters, Y-E-S?"

Dr. Bak Nguyen

1646
FROM HOW TO NOT FAIL AS A DENTIST
"To leverage means to buy time."

Dr. Bak Nguyen

1647
FROM HOW TO NOT FAIL AS A DENTIST
"Emotional intelligence is the key to advancement."

Dr. Bak Nguyen

1648
FROM MINDSET ARMORY
"Every time the wind blows in my face, what I really feel is the speed of freedom, the velocity of potential and the freshness of her love."

Dr. Bak Nguyen

1649
FROM MINDSET ARMORY
"In everyday life, this is called EMPATHY, SYMPATHY and being RESOURCEFUL."

Dr. Bak Nguyen

1650
FROM MINDSET ARMORY
"Only by being KIND can one truly listen."

Dr. Bak Nguyen

1651
FROM HUMILITY FOR SUCCESS
"Just like Kindness is often misunderstood for Weakness from the small-minded people, Humility is too often misinterpreted for submission."
Dr. Bak Nguyen

1652
FROM HUMILITY FOR SUCCESS
"Influence is power without weakness."
Dr. Bak Nguyen

1653
FROM HUMILITY FOR SUCCESS
"Influence is enforced with love, kindness and vision, not fear, authority and force as power often is."
Dr. Bak Nguyen

1654
FROM HUMILITY FOR SUCCESS
"Speed and acceleration counter balance motion sickness."
Dr. Bak Nguyen

1655
FROM HUMILITY FOR SUCCESS
"Nuance is the essence of Humility."
Dr. Bak Nguyen

1656
FROM HUMILITY FOR SUCCESS
"If you wanted the secret of living forever,
try Flexibility."
Dr. Bak Nguyen

1657
FROM HUMILITY FOR SUCCESS
"Flexibility is the capability to adapt and to leverage the changing conditions to move forward. It is never stable, but it does not have to be rocky."
Dr. Bak Nguyen

1658
FROM HUMILITY FOR SUCCESS
"I found many of my powers
in the service of others."
Dr. Bak Nguyen

1659
FROM HUMILITY FOR SUCCESS
"To unbalance is to move forward.
To harmonize that rise is my new wisdom."
Dr. Bak Nguyen

1660
FROM HUMILITY FOR SUCCESS
"Humility is what keeps us relevant…"
Dr. Bak Nguyen

1661
FROM MASTERMIND
"The fun and the thrill keep me going,
especially while in the hardest spots."
Dr. Bak Nguyen

1662
FROM MASTERMIND
"In financial vocabulary, power is mainly
a big liability!"
Dr. Bak Nguyen

1663
FROM MASTERMIND
"I do not balance, I leverage."
Dr. Bak Nguyen

1664
FROM MASTERMIND
"To enhance your power, find your worth."
Dr. Bak Nguyen

1665
FROM MASTERMIND
"Discipline will breakdown mountains, a rock at a time."
Dr. Bak Nguyen

1666
FROM THE ENERGY FORMULA
"For a MOMENTUM to happen, I need all 3 components to play in my favour, DESIRE, VALUES and WILL."
Dr. Bak Nguyen

1667
FROM THE ENERGY FORMULA
"Therefore, for your own success, never confuse Potential and Kinetic. Both are Energy, but one is talk, the other is walk."
Dr. Bak Nguyen

1668
FROM THE ENERGY FORMULA
"There is no good or bad Energy, Energy is Energy."
Dr. Bak Nguyen

1669
FROM THE ENERGY FORMULA
"Act, learn, be kind, adapt and keep pushing. This is canalization."
Dr. Bak Nguyen

1670
FROM THE ENERGY FORMULA
"Oh yes, this is a numbers' game. Energy is quantitative, much more than it is qualitative."
Dr. Bak Nguyen

1671
FROM PLAYBOOK INTRODUCTION VOLUME 1
"You will fail, how fast and how often, it is up to you! But the more you fail, the wiser and stronger you'll get."
Dr. Bak Nguyen

1672
FROM PLAYBOOK INTRODUCTION VOLUME 1
"If you want to bend the rules and to paint your own reality, keep moving, faster and faster!"
Dr. Bak Nguyen

1673
FROM AMONGST THE ALPHAS, VOLUME 1
"With Humility, we will make the most of the gift of Creativity without the shadow of pride."
Dr. Bak Nguyen

1674
FROM SUCCESS IS A CHOICE
"Flexibility is what will keep your heart young, your mind sharp and your power exponential."
Dr. Bak Nguyen

1675
FROM MIRRORS
"Mentorship is a path to power and influence."
Dr. Bak Nguyen

1676
FROM MIRRORS
"Respect, real respect is the most influential attitude one may show.
Dr. Bak Nguyen

1677
FROM MIRRORS
"Only once you know your boundaries can you truly start to challenge them and find power beyond."
Dr. Bak Nguyen

1678
FROM MIRRORS
"From attraction, one needs to evolve into a centre of gravity."
Dr. Bak Nguyen

1679
FROM MIRRORS
"Control allows to keep doubt in line."
Dr. Bak Nguyen

1680
FROM MIRRORS
"Control is mainly both a strength and weakness at the same time."
Dr. Bak Nguyen

1681
FROM MIRRORS
"Self-control, that's the real power within."
Dr. Bak Nguyen

1682
FROM MIRRORS
"Every time that one is applying control, one is giving away part of its freedom, therefore,
part of his happiness."
Dr. Bak Nguyen

1683
FROM MIRRORS
"The power of the human will is to reshape the perception of the universe as desired."
Dr. Bak Nguyen

1684
FROM MIRRORS
"Awareness is the beginning of our legend."
Dr. Bak Nguyen

1685
FROM MIRRORS
"The shortcut to power is awareness, true and complete awareness of oneself."
Dr. Bak Nguyen

1686
FROM MIRRORS
"To attract is to tune in with
the frequency of the Universe."
Dr. Bak Nguyen

1687
FROM MIRRORS
"It takes only one heart to believe in me for me to love. By the second and third ones, true power emerges from within, and I became, not only attraction but a Centre of Gravity."
Dr. Bak Nguyen

1688
FROM SUCCESS IS A CHOICE
"To break free without pain nor resistance, look for the point of inflexion and boost your current speed."
Dr. Bak Nguyen

1689
FROM SUCCESS IS A CHOICE
"To each force its counterbalance.
To evolution, mine was Speed."
Dr. Bak Nguyen

1690
FROM SUCCESS IS A CHOICE
"Leveraging is a question of mindset."
Dr. Bak Nguyen

1691
FROM SUCCESS IS A CHOICE
"Leverage is not gambling, it is thinking and improving the odds while speeding up."
Dr. Bak Nguyen

1692
FROM RISING
"If you want to beat time, you need to learn to leverage."
Dr. Bak Nguyen

1693
FROM RISING
"Once you've accepted the game, the one in control is the one provoking the events."
Dr. Bak Nguyen

1694
FROM RISING
"The heart act, the mind reacts. This is a beautiful and winning combination."
Dr. Bak Nguyen

1695
FROM RISING
"To gain more control rise up, loose that control!"
Dr. Bak Nguyen

1696
FROM RISING
"Whatever your reality, all the theorems, strategies and laws you may found will reinforce that reality."
Dr. Bak Nguyen

1697
FROM RISING
"GREED has to serve FEAR, that's the only way to advance with least resistance."
Dr. Bak Nguyen

1698
FROM RISING
"No rise comes without friction.
If it does, it simply not a rise."
Dr. Bak Nguyen

1699
FROM RISING
"Influence will cut through resistance like a hot knife through butter."
Dr. Bak Nguyen

1700
FROM RISING
"Influence is immaterial, it can be obtained, divided, and yet, multiplied."
Dr. Bak Nguyen

1701
FROM AFTERMATH
"Let GREED be the force for change, good and sustainable change. GREED will make it last and will spread it throughout the world."
Dr. Bak Nguyen

1702
FROM AFTERMATH
"The best remedy to FEAR is GREED. So, in the lack of a better word, let's leverage our GREED for the greater good!"
Dr. Bak Nguyen

1703
FROM AFTERMATH
"Philanthropy is leverage and social impact, not charity."
Dr. Bak Nguyen

1704
FROM RELEVANCY
"The wording isn't the surface, but the path to a much, much deeper truth, our of identity."
Dr. Bak Nguyen

1705
FROM RELEVANCY
"To be flexible and to adapt again and again…"
Dr. Bak Nguyen

1706
FROM RELEVANCY
"Give because you can, not because you care."
Dr. Bak Nguyen

1707
FROM THE POWER OF DR
"Drive is resilience combined with will power."
Dr. Bak Nguyen

1708
FROM THE POWER OF DR
"Power is a chain, not a station."
Dr. Bak Nguyen

1709
FROM THE POWER OF DR
"It is mind-blowing where you can go once you have yielded both humility and nobility!"
Dr. Bak Nguyen

1710
FROM TORNADO
"The key is emotion through repetition."
Dr. Bak Nguyen

1711
FROM TORNADO
"THE POWER OF THE DRAGON did not bring my invisibility as describe in the book, it elevated me to powers I never even dreamt of."
Dr. Bak Nguyen

1712
FROM TORNADO
"Dreaming, keep dreaming, and if you believe enough to walk, well, your Momentum will bring you the means to reach all of your dreams."
Dr. Bak Nguyen

1713
FROM TORNADO
"Dream, believe, share to connect and enjoy the ride fuelling your Momentum."
Dr. Bak Nguyen

1714
FROM TORNADO
"Forget impacting, look for flowing instead."
Dr. Bak Nguyen

1715
FROM TORNADO
"A Momentum, just like a tornado is a natural phenomenon of nature."
Dr. Bak Nguyen

1716
FROM EMPOWERMENT
"I act, I contain my consequences and, even before the reaction, I am reacting to my own actions and consequences. This is the essence of my speed."
Dr. Bak Nguyen

1717
FROM EMPOWERMENT
"In my quest for knowledge, I found my power in helping others."
Dr. Bak Nguyen

1718
FROM EMPOWERMENT
"The mirror effect has many facets. Resistance isn't one of them."
Dr. Bak Nguyen

1719
FROM THE MODERN WOMAN
"The real power isn't control, but influence!"
Dr. Bak Nguyen

1720
FROM THE MODERN WOMAN

"Mentorship is not about knowledge, but about kindness, vision and sustainability."

Dr. Bak Nguyen

1721
FROM BOOTCAMP

"Forget good and bad, the world is not linear. Look for cause and effect, those are from the ripple effects."

Dr. Bak Nguyen

1722
FROM THE UAX STORY

"Everything revolves around emotions."

Dr. Bak Nguyen

1723
FROM THE UAX STORY

"Viva the Power of Yes!"

Dr. Bak Nguyen

1724
FROM THE UAX STORY
"Sharing is the way to grow.
Elevating is the way to fly."

Dr. Bak Nguyen

1725
FROM TOUCHSTONE, LEVERAGING TODAY'S PSYCHOLOGICAL SMOG
"Nature has designed STRESS as a stimulus. We, we have made it our by default response to the stimulus itself."

Dr. Bak Nguyen

1726
FROM TOUCHSTONE, LEVERAGING TODAY'S PSYCHOLOGICAL SMOG
"Speed is the answer to avoid the touchstone of FAILURE."

Dr. Bak Nguyen

1727
FROM TOUCHSTONE, LEVERAGING TODAY'S PSYCHOLOGICAL SMOG
"Tension and pressure are forces that you feel. How do you experience it is about your speed and position on the lane."

Dr. Bak Nguyen

1728
FROM ALPHA LADDERS VOLUME ONE
"Trust your instincts, because reason and sight will always be late in the game of perception... if they aver get there."
Dr. Bak Nguyen

1729
FROM ALPHA LADDERS VOLUME ONE
"Share to live forever!"
Dr. Bak Nguyen

1730
FROM ALPHA LADDERS VOLUME ONE
"With a confident and gentle core, empty to be available, this is how I became the legend of Dr. Bak, AKA the Tornado."
Dr. Bak Nguyen

1731
FROM ALPHA LADDERS VOLUME ONE
"Power, to last through time and space has at its core compassion, the passion for others."
Dr. Bak Nguyen

1732
FROM POWERPLAY
"The most powerful of leverage is when you can borrow time and repay it with the interests you made, borrowing it!"

Dr. Bak Nguyen

1733
FROM 1SELF
"Influence is power without resistance."

Dr. Bak Nguyen

1734
FROM THE BOOK OF LEGENDS VOLUME 3
"To gain depth, give it everything that you have, and then, detach yourself completely to react honestly to what you've created."

Dr. Bak Nguyen

1735
FROM THE BOOK OF LEGENDS VOLUME 3
"When things are going well, do not wait, double down on the deployment. Those are the seeds to your Momentum."

Dr. Bak Nguyen

1736
FROM THE BOOK OF LEGENDS VOLUME 3
"Less identity, less constraints, more possibilities."
Dr. Bak Nguyen

1737
FROM THE BOOK OF LEGENDS VOLUME 3
"Creativity is about fun. Fun is about speed and ease."
Dr. Bak Nguyen

1738
FROM THE CONFESSION OF AN OVERACHIEVER
"Listen to your needs and leverage your hormones."
Dr. Bak Nguyen

1739
FROM THE CONFESSION OF AN OVERACHIEVER
"Feed your hunger, then grow enough to feed even the hunger of others. You just found power."
Dr. Bak Nguyen

1740
FROM TO OVERACHIEVE EVERYTHING BEING LAZY
"Enjoy your dreams first, only then, you may engage and empower them."
Dr. Bak Nguyen

This is **Shortcut volume 6, POWER**. Welcome to the Alphas.

Hammering air three times over
and it will become steel.

Dr. BAK NGUYEN

PART 3
"LIFE"
by Dr. BAK NGUYEN

Life is about the journeys that we are walking. I would love to say that it is a question of choices but that would not be completely true. Is it? Until now, in the journeys of the **SHORTCUT series**, we addressed much of the how to move forward. This is about the what and what if.

Is Life a choice? It is now. What are you doing next, when and how are all legitimate questions that you are either asking yourself or running away from. That's your choice.

> "Choices start with awareness.
> Sooner or later, the sleeper must awake."
> Dr. Bak Nguyen

That's quote #2508. That awakening, we all go through with it, it is called the **Quest of Identity**. If the choices were made for you until then, well, with your identity, you are making your own. To accept and face or to be in denial will be your choice to make.

Abraham Maslow describes very clearly the journey of our lives with the Pyramid of Maslow.

SELF-ACTUALIZATION
ESTEEM
LOVE/BELONGING
SAFETY
`PHYSIOLOGICAL NEEDS`

THE PYRAMID OF ABRAHAM MASLOW

If hunger, sex, and security were our basic goals, as we are born, these have been chosen for us and set by default, by our parents, by society, by Conformity. These are called security and stability. No system is perfect and whatever we made think of these systems, we should be grateful for its protection.

But just like our body is awakening and changing with the emergence of the sexual hormones at the teen's age, our spirit will eventually awaken and be looking for more too. These 2 awakenings may coincide, but very quickly, after the sexual awakening has passed its peak, most of us, fell back into stability and security, finding our place in society.

We might have found our sexual identity, a soul mate, a position, and even a purpose but all of these will be defined within the constraint of society. Well, awake, we were looking for our place in life, society was just a step.

Then, a second drastic change in hormones will occur as we become parents. Even if the process is different for the women and the men, both genders, as they are taking care of a newborn, will experience a change in hormones and purpose.

This will start the division between life as a man and life as a woman. If society told us how to behave until then, we found our own way as we became a couple. For a few years, we were in symbiosis... until our hormones reminded us of how different we are.

Many will say that it is at motherhood that a woman truly becomes a woman. We can't say as much about men... some will take much longer before the transformation... Don't be too quick to judge, it was physiological, hormonal.

Having experienced the first half of Life (I am 44 at the time of this writing), I can tell you that the same story happens again and again, not just as a pattern but as a code imprinted in our DNA. I was looking at my son growing and changing, almost on auto-pilot. He is growing and reacting to the changes happening inside of him. The questions are always the same: "so now what?" and "what's next?".

Surprisingly, **WHY** is not one of these classic and embed questions. **WHAT** is. Then, I looked at my parents and grandparents to see how they have answered these questions. Even if they went through 2 wars and had to rebuild their lives, not once but twice, within 2 generations' time, they each faced the same questions.

What was different was how they answered these questions, how and how fast. War was a context, often an excuse but never an eraser of these questions, for as long as they were alive and flowing with hormones. They felt, made their choices, and faced the consequences.

Fortunately for me, I was born after the facts, after the wars. I was born in security as my family was grinding to regain stability in a new country. For that, I will be eternally grateful. That explained much of the **IMMIGRANT** theme I used in my books.

Grinding and busy gaining back what was lost, I was pushed into performing to earn a place in their new society, new for them, mine as I was concerned. With pressure and results, I had a different childhood but my hormonal change happened as programmed. Just like my son is going through his, with comfort and status.

I went from surviving to thriving. I worked hard and delivered as asked by my family, by society and I rose, from security to comfort, from stability to status. These were all my parents ever dream for their children... but that did not interfere with our hormones and awakening. And then, I became a father.

As a man becoming a father, I experienced many internal changes. Most of which forced me to review all these choices I made by default. I wanted the best for my son. To give him the best, I needed to be the best first.

Fortunately for me, I was raised well and building from the shoulders of my parents and grandparents. I will even say that I was a child of society since everything that I was until that point, was a successful *product* of society. That brought me comfort and status. I am grateful.

Just like my parents and grandparents, me too, I will have to lead the way for my son, not just to protect him but to empower him to his full potential. And there is when the shift happened.

My parents were looking to provide security and to regain lost status. They were looking for security and stability. Me, on the other hand, I having been spared the burden of war, I was looking for freedom and opportunity. That was a drastic shift in mentality.

None of that mattered to my son and his evolution. Like me, he grew up surrounded by love and warmth. My parents had not much and yet, I was feeling rich and loved. My son, he has everything, and he too, felt rich and loved. My parents had templates of life for me to follow. I am trying to discover new ones walking life, as my son is walking by my side.

Then, as I grew older, I got through my midlife crisis, from the surge and craving for hormones. That was messy but it put everything back in perspective. Looking to understand the choices that I faced, I, once more looked at my parents and grandparents.

War set my father back for about 20 years. His midlife crisis happened too, but much later in life, as he was retiring after a great life of hard work and catch up. He too had to face his hormones after the rush of adrenaline, only he has less time and fewer hormones to run with. But the emotions were pretty similar.

By then, my grandparents have passed away. I loved my grandparents, the parents of my mother, as much as parents. At their passing, to mourn, I went back through their stories and their choices. They faced the same challenges as their children but somehow made it differently.

By the second emigration, losing their home and status a second time, they settled with more ease. They were ahead of their kids… Younger, I felt like a prince in their company, and yet, all they had was the experience to face their choices and its consequences.

How they see Life impacted how they feel inside. And they built with these hormones, of how they felt inside. They have experienced sadness and losses more than once and yet, you can feel the security in their eye. My grandfather and my mom had a picture on the front page of an old newspaper announcing the arrival of Vietnamese refugees in Guam.

Well, I had to read the title to understand. With my grandfather's smile, they looked like they were going out from a cruise boat from the Bahamas. This is how strong his spirit was.

And then, he too, had to face illness and age. He too, had his hormones changed. His death made a hole in my soul. From that hole, I gained much perspective, one at my own future.

> "The map of our journey is derived from our hormones. And that journey is a common template."
> Dr. Bak Nguyen

That's the 2509th quote. So I had 4 generations to learn from, between my grandfather and myself, from my father to my son, I found the pattern of Life: the hormonal map.

Each will have their choices and will walk theirs consequences. But we all had, do, and will. As strong will as one can be, we are the products of what we are perceiving from the outside world. In other words, we are reacting to how we feel inside, from the hormones that our body releases. There is no exception to that rule.

From war to wealth, love and jealousy were the same, only the templates vary. From surviving to thriving, the wording changed but the hormones were, at the end of the day, the same, from our DNA.

I hate to think that my life is pre-written but, at the same time, it would be a denial of my part not to see the patterns emerging despite the large difference in circumstances.

> "Feelings, choices, and hormones.
> These will define our lives."
> **Dr. Bak Nguyen**

That's the 2510th quote. Well, the quotes you will be reading is what I found walking the consequences of my choices and the remnant of the choices of my parents and grandparents. That's legacy.

If the hormones and the feelings can be changed, we still have the choices of our answers, of how to react, and how fast. And these are what I am sharing with you. We are not in control of 2/3 of this equation but somehow, with awareness, we can paint a much different life.

I should have started the **SHORTCUT series** with these quotes **LIFE**, but to me, **HEALING** was more important (focused on actions). **LIFE** is the journey and this is the mapping of what will happen. I included **LIFE** in the volume of **POWER** because to walk Life and to derive from its heavy tendencies is not an easy thing.

And yet, with only 1/3 of the equation, we can make a difference. For that, we need **Confidence** and the yielding of each of the powers that we will find on the way.

Between the hormonal map and the pyramid of Maslow (psychological map) you now have a very clear trajectory of what is ahead. Knowing, you are now gaining a little more from these 2/3 of the equation, not in your control.

This is **Shortcut volume 6, POWER**. Welcome to the Alphas.

*Hammering air three times over
and it will become steel.*
Dr. BAK NGUYEN

PART 4
"73 LIFE QUOTES"
by Dr. BAK NGUYEN

0214
FROM SYMPHONY OF SKILLS
"Don't put yourself on top!
Take your breath at the top!"
Dr. Bak Nguyen

0215
FROM SYMPHONY OF SKILLS
"To live a dream is the dream of a lifetime."
Dr. Bak Nguyen

0216
FROM LEADERSHIP, PANDORA'S BOX
"Life and creativity come from the interaction
of two strong opposites."
Dr. Bak Nguyen

0217
FROM LEADERSHIP, PANDORA'S BOX
"So don't judge, since you'll be judging yourself!"
Dr. Bak Nguyen

0218
FROM LEADERSHIP, PANDORA'S BOX
"Life is a journey, a Journey of Empowerment."
Dr. Bak Nguyen

0219
FROM LEADERSHIP, PANDORA'S BOX
"Gratitude tells much about one's character.
If there is no Gratitude, there is no hope and therefore, no future."
Dr. Bak Nguyen

0220
FROM LEADERSHIP, PANDORA'S BOX
"If we embrace the kingdom of Gratitude,
we have the map that will lead us back to paradise."
Dr. Bak Nguyen

0221
FROM LEADERSHIP, PANDORA'S BOX
" Our world is not black and white nor good or bad.
We made sure of that, by adapting."
Dr. Bak Nguyen

0222
FROM LEADERSHIP, PANDORA'S BOX
"Life is free. Our birth's right is liberty.
We started life with our legacy."
Dr. Bak Nguyen

0223
FROM LEADERSHIP, PANDORA'S BOX
"We are what we eat, so is the fire of life."
Dr. Bak Nguyen

0224
FROM LEADERSHIP, PANDORA'S BOX
"To each force, it is a nemesis to keep the balance. From the reaction between the opposites derives the energy of the universe, we call it vitality."
Dr. Bak Nguyen

0225
FROM LEADERSHIP, PANDORA'S BOX
"Life can be about us if we make it about others first."
Dr. Bak Nguyen

0226
FROM IDENTITY, ANTHOLOGY OF QUESTS
"Harmony is fluid, it is magical, it is the natural state of life."
Dr. Bak Nguyen

0227
FROM IDENTITY, ANTHOLOGY OF QUESTS
"Life is like music, there are many notes,
but each note is unique and precise.
We all know when we hit it right!"
Dr. Bak Nguyen

0228
FROM IDENTITY, ANTHOLOGY OF QUESTS
"Sometime the only way to see is
with your eyes close."
Dr. Bak Nguyen

0229
FROM IDENTITY, ANTHOLOGY OF QUESTS
"The trees will not have gave up everything.
They will have traded in freedom for security, passion
for longevity and adventure for knowledge...,
not wisdom, since wisdom is from experience."
Dr. Bak Nguyen

0230
FROM IDENTITY, ANTHOLOGY OF QUESTS
"The more we see and understand of life,
the harder it will be to simply eat and replenish."
Dr. Bak Nguyen

0231
FROM IDENTITY, ANTHOLOGY OF QUESTS
"Emotions are the chords of life."
Dr. Bak Nguyen

0232
FROM IDENTITY, ANTHOLOGY OF QUESTS
"And life is kind, life have provided us such beauties to chase, to each, our taste!"
Dr. Bak Nguyen

0233
FROM IDENTITY, ANTHOLOGY OF QUESTS
"Emotions are like maths, precise and not negotiable."
Dr. Bak Nguyen

0234
FROM IDENTITY, ANTHOLOGY OF QUESTS
"The core of the song of life is in the rhythm and the chords, not the lyrics."
Dr. Bak Nguyen

0235
FROM CHANGING THE WORLD FROM A DENTAL CHAIR
" Life is dynamic, it is a permanent state of reorganization. So is the market."
Dr. Bak Nguyen

0236
FROM THE POWER BEHIND THE ALPHA
" Life is running its course, so are we."
Dr. Bak Nguyen

0237
FROM MOMENTUM TRANSFER
" Perfection is a lie. Everything, to exist, has two faces, one dark, the another, light. What oscillates in between, we call life."
Dr. Bak Nguyen

0238
FROM HYBRID
"Chords, patterns, templates, tempo, and rhythm are the keys to every song, to every situation."
Dr. Bak Nguyen

0239
FROM HYBRID
"Hunger is good. Hunger is vital."
Dr. Bak Nguyen

0240
FROM HYBRID
"Desire is the greed for life."
Dr. Bak Nguyen

0241
FROM HYBRID
"Curiosity will keep us aware of the wealth of beauty of our legacy, Life."
Dr. Bak Nguyen

0242
FROM REBOOT, TO GROW FROM MIDLIFE CRISIS
"Not everything that goes up needs to come back down if we can be wise and flexible about it."
Dr. Bak Nguyen

0243
FROM REBOOT, TO GROW FROM MIDLIFE CRISIS
"Life is all about choices."
Dr. Bak Nguyen

0244
FROM REBOOT, TO GROW FROM MIDLIFE CRISIS
"Everything in Life is about choice and awareness."
Dr. Bak Nguyen

0245
FROM SELFMADE
"Life showed me the way, I simply followed with Hope and passion."
Dr. Bak Nguyen

0246
FROM SELFMADE
"Win and enjoy, but keep pushing, the real victory is in the long term."
Dr. Bak Nguyen

0247
FROM SELFMADE
"It was all a matter of openness."
Dr. Bak Nguyen

0248
FROM THE RISE OF THE UNICORN
"Any journey will change you, good or bad."
Dr. Bak Nguyen

0249
FROM HOW TO WRITE A BOOK IN 30 DAYS
"It's not easy to change the world. Even when you do good, someday it feels like the world doesn't bother much."

Dr. Bak Nguyen

0250
FROM KRYPTO
"Life is not about fairness, but at least, everyone should have a fair chance to succeed, no?"

Dr. Bak Nguyen

0251
FROM KRYPTO
"Life is about love. love is all about taking and having chances. A second, a third, a fifth… where there is love, there is life."

Dr. Bak Nguyen

0252
FROM HORIZON VOLUME ONE
"Life and Time are borrowed goods. Make the most of out them before it is too late."

Dr. Bak Nguyen

0253
FROM THE POWER OF YES, VOLUME 1
"Nothing is free in life. One only chooses what price to pay, and for what."

Dr. Bak Nguyen

0254
FROM THE POWER OF YES, VOLUME 1
"Life is really about the choices you are making."

Dr. Bak Nguyen

0255
FROM HORIZON VOLUME TWO
"Being open to life and the opportunities, you never know what life will greet you with."

Dr. Bak Nguyen

0256
FROM HORIZON VOLUME TWO
"Life is what it is. Our story is how we react to it. Legendary is when we become one with of the Flow of Life."

Dr. Bak Nguyen

0257
FROM HOW TO NOT FAIL AS A DENTIST
"You might own things, but in reality,
you owe everything."

Dr. Bak Nguyen

0258
FROM MINDSET ARMORY
"Balance is life. The life of a hero is to unbalance and to keep the scale toward Life, until Death feeling cheated come back to claim its due."

Dr. Bak Nguyen

0259
FROM MINDSET ARMORY
"You can't cheat Death, but can gave her the run of her life, making her feel what it's like to be human, with the emotions and hormones, with Greed and Fear."

Dr. Bak Nguyen

0260
FROM HUMILITY FOR SUCCESS
"Life is always created from the interaction of opposites. The stronger the oppositions, the bigger the life."

Dr. Bak Nguyen

0261
FROM PLAYBOOK INTRODUCTION VOLUME 1
"Luck is a very capricious creature."
Dr. Bak Nguyen

0262
FROM AMONGST THE ALPHAS, VOLUME 1
"Amongst people, we try to connect. Amongst peers, it is simply too hard to resist, once we connected, then we start to compare."
Dr. Bak Nguyen

0263
FROM AMONGST THE ALPHAS, VOLUME 1
"One always sees what one chooses to see, nothing else."
Dr. Bak Nguyen

0264
FROM AMONGST THE ALPHAS, VOLUME 1
"Judging is painful."
Dr. Bak Nguyen

0265
FROM AMONGST THE ALPHAS, VOLUME 1
"Good or bad, most relationships are about us and our perception, not about the other party."
Dr. Bak Nguyen

0266
FROM AMONGST THE ALPHAS, VOLUME 1
"Pride is to protect with all of yourself, your vulnerabilities."
Dr. Bak Nguyen

0267
FROM AMONGST THE ALPHAS, VOLUME 1
"Craving for control is the best patch of insecurity."
Dr. Bak Nguyen

0268
FROM AMONGST THE ALPHAS, VOLUME 1
"The recipe is always the same: less pain, less identity, less pride, more results."
Dr. Bak Nguyen

0269
FROM AMONGST THE ALPHAS, VOLUME 1
"Sacrifice is a word of those victims of the world, not those drafting it."
Dr. Bak Nguyen

0270
FROM AMONGST THE ALPHAS, VOLUME 1
"The more I write, the more I learn,
the more I have to share."
Dr. Bak Nguyen

0271
FROM AMONGST THE ALPHAS, VOLUME 1
"Gratitude and fear don't mix well.
The more grateful you are,
the less fearful you'll grow."
Dr. Bak Nguyen

0272
FROM AMONGST THE ALPHAS, VOLUME 1
"The bigger part of Life is about balance and harmony, living and dying, not just fighting to live nor dying to survive."
Dr. Bak Nguyen

0273
FROM AMONGST THE ALPHAS, VOLUME 2
"Naivety can be cruel and hurt even
more than madness."
Dr. Bak Nguyen

0274
FROM AMONGST THE ALPHAS, VOLUME 2
"When you dance with the winds, you are a fool to try to control them, just follow the flow and enjoy the dance."
Dr. Bak Nguyen

0275
FROM AMONGST THE ALPHAS, VOLUME 2
"Smaller the minds, lesser the mistakes…"
Dr. Bak Nguyen

0276
FROM SUCCESS IS A CHOICE
"Well, life is not about being fair, but being smart, about being wise."
Dr. Bak Nguyen

0277
FROM SUCCESS IS A CHOICE
"Not everything in Life is a problem to be fixed."
Dr. Bak Nguyen

0278
FROM RISING
"Nothing is set in stone, put that through your head, the sooner, the less painful your journey will be!"
Dr. Bak Nguyen

0279
FROM TORNADO
"Emotions are the natural energy contained within each of us."
Dr. Bak Nguyen

0280
FROM BOOTCAMP
"On paper, perfection is king, not in life."
Dr. Bak Nguyen

0281
FROM TOUCHSTONE, LEVERAGING TODAY'S PSYCHOLOGICAL SMOG
"Life is dynamic, moving, always morphing, and never standing still. If not, we wouldn't be calling it Life."
Dr. Bak Nguyen

0282
FROM TOUCHSTONE, LEVERAGING TODAY'S PSYCHOLOGICAL SMOG
"Fighting Life or running from it, where would it lead? To the opposite of Life…"
Dr. Bak Nguyen

0283
FROM TOUCHSTONE, LEVERAGING TODAY'S PSYCHOLOGICAL SMOG
"Embrace Life and see it as an opportunity. That's your leverage."

Dr. Bak Nguyen

0284
FROM TOUCHSTONE, LEVERAGING TODAY'S PSYCHOLOGICAL SMOG
"Your perspective of Life will define the degree of stress you are experimenting with."

Dr. Bak Nguyen

0285
FROM 1SELF
"The Universe is a dynamic balancing the forces. You have to decide what you are in that dynamic, a force, or an effect."

Dr. Bak Nguyen

0286
FROM MIRRORS
"To see life black or white is a choice, not a truth nor a science."

Dr. Bak Nguyen

This is **Shortcut volume 6, POWER**. Welcome to the Alphas.

*Hammering air three times over
and it will become steel.*
Dr. BAK NGUYEN

PART 5
"TIME"
by Dr. BAK NGUYEN

Time, that's our most precious resource.
Health is Time,
Wealth is Time,

Pain and sorrow fade with Time.
And of course, Time is money.
So Life is Time.

So what is Time doing in a book about power? Well, since the beginning of my writing, very earlier on, I introduced the concept of leveraging in the mindsets that I shared with you.

As I was writing **TOUCHSTONE** with Dr. Ken Serota, he mentioned that I have a very particular way to use the word leverage as leverage and not as a financial tool. I must say that I was surprised by the comment, I never thought that my wording was that different.

Coming from the financial field and the personal growth as I completed my formal education with books and conferences, to me, to leverage seems natural. That's not the case for most people. Dr. Serota pointed that out clearly.

Then, as I introduced the concept of leveraging, the first time that it found its way into my quotes was as leveraging liabilities.

> "Leverage your liabilities into assets
> to always move forward."
> Dr. Bak Nguyen

That is absolutely true. But most of the time, we are more inclined to avoid our liabilities than to leverage and face them. And yet, we can still leverage every day. So what are we leveraging? Time, mostly. Time is what we all have and Time is what we must learn to leverage.

Younger, we had more Time and did not appreciate the resource as we should. We had so much Time available that Society invented school and class to keep us busy. Then, we learnt to exchange our Time for money, taking jobs and contracts, we all did.

Some of us will do that for most of our lives with the promise that, eventually, we won't have to work anymore and that we will finally have free time. And free time, that must mean happiness! That's the dream, that's the promise.

Unfortunately, many of us will be fooled by that promise and might never find happiness, even with much free time. Why? Because by retirement, some will fall into depression and illness, eating up all of the free time that they just found.

Some will go as far as to say that it was the free time and the boredom that made them sick. Is that an exaggeration? Well, as doctors, we diagnose and treat the illnesses and the wounds, not always do we establish the cause-effect relationship between how an illness came to appear. I am a doctor and I will respect that art and science.

That said, I am a doctor and studied the human body most of my adult life. I know that we are reacting to the hormones that our bodies produce. Actually, we are the product of our hormones. In other words, we are what we feel and we act accordingly.

That said, what happens when you have a body full of hormones and you shift most of it abruptly, going from busy to free? Your body will react. An no two bodies will have the exact same reaction. This is a fact and something much harder to identify as the illness might appear only years later as your body craved.

But it is not because our science and medicine do not make the correlation that it is not true. Our body is aging, we already have to deal with that. Now, if we cease or decrease the production of certain key hormones we were running on for years, our body will have to cope with that missing component too! So no, free time is not always the answer.

Instead, it is what are we doing with the time that we are given that will make us happy or not. I know, we each have our own definition of happiness but it starts with the awareness that we are in control and that we have time to act.

If you are ready, you will be putting time and energy into good use and harness its power and the satisfaction of your results. That's will keep you very happy and busy. If you are not ready yet, that's okay too but time is still flowing, only not in your favour! And your happiness is fading away with that **flow of Time**...

So time is our most precious resource. You can be rich or poor, you still have the same 24 hours available. Young and old will be the difference here, and as such, we each had our turn of youth, so it was pretty fair! Being healthy or sick, this will be the next issue of dealing with time. On that, we have to deal with what is given.

And about wealth? Well, every self made millionaire will tell you that time, with the right mindset and discipline in place, allowed them to reach their status. Time is always the key factor.

And what to say about doctors and healing. After a surgical intervention, once again, everything heals with time, body, and mind. So yes, Time is our most precious resource.

Moving forward are the quotes and wisdom that I understood as I was looking for more wins, jumping from win to win. I started with the impression that Time is a Force of Nature that I have to beat.

For most of my early life, I relentlessly sought ways to cheat time. And the answer was always found within **SPEED**, speed and efficiency. That was still the time that I would break each wall put in front of me.

Then, as I grew older and a little wiser, I stop seeking confrontation and knocking down walls. I am still pretty good at it but it is too exhausting to fight on all fronts, all the time. So I today will do my best to avoid direct confrontation and to seek alternatives instead. I will not back down from a fight but, today, I will do my best to reconcile first.

> "Victory is simply not a win if the price is too high or the delay too long."
> Dr. Bak Nguyen

That's quote #2511. So I took the same approach with **Time**. Today Time is more a companion that I will try to beat in a friendly race than a battle to the death.

To face Time, I bet on Speed. Since the beginning of my **Quest of Identity**, I bet on speed to reach the next win, the next checkpoint, to catch my breath, and to score a win against Time.

Time is a formidable rival. Don't get me wrong on that. But Time can also be leveraged and help you reach your next goal with impact and power.

> "To always race against Time, I killed procrastination in its bed. And that was the end of that story."
> Dr. Bak Nguyen

That's quote #2512. I empowered my speed to reach heights that will impress even Time. And this is how I find my worth nowadays, not looking in the mirror or thirsty of the opinion of my peers but looking at my reflection in the eyes of Time and the other Forces of Nature.

About the Forces of Nature, my 15th book bears that same title. If you have interests, you can read about the other Forces of Nature influencing our lives. Time is one of them.

And here they come next, 67 quotes on and about Time. If there is one prominent theme, it is **leverage**, how to leverage Time to propel yourself higher, further, and faster.

This is **Shortcut volume 6, POWER**. Welcome to the Alphas.

Dr. BAK NGUYEN

PART 6
"67 TIME QUOTES"
by Dr. BAK NGUYEN

0287
FROM SYMPHONY OF SKILLS
"You can't change the past.
You can only influence the future."
Dr. Bak Nguyen

0288
FROM LEADERSHIP, PANDORA'S BOX
"We cannot change what was.
We can only have the wisdom to ease the way."
Dr. Bak Nguyen

0289
FROM LEADERSHIP, PANDORA'S BOX
"Cheating is bad, but cheating death
can be uplifting!"
Dr. Bak Nguyen

0290
FROM LEADERSHIP, PANDORA'S BOX
"The fear of Death is worse than Death itself."
Dr. Bak Nguyen

0291
FROM LEADERSHIP, PANDORA'S BOX
"Death is a sure thing. But when, that's not written yet, not until it's too late. So why care?"
Dr. Bak Nguyen

0292
FROM LEADERSHIP, PANDORA'S BOX
"From the past, only ghosts and shadows are heroes."
Dr. Bak Nguyen

0293
FROM AMONGST THE ALPHAS, VOLUME 1
"The day that I won't be able to move forward, I've died a year earlier!"
Dr. Bak Nguyen

0294
FROM AMONGST THE ALPHAS, VOLUME 2
"You wanted to live forever. Well, stay humble!"
Dr. Bak Nguyen

0295
FROM IDENTITY, ANTHOLOGY OF QUESTS
"We are all borrowers. Time, money, talents."
Dr. Bak Nguyen

0296
FROM IDENTITY, ANTHOLOGY OF QUESTS
"Time is circular and dynamic. It can be paced and outran for a while. Only a while..."
Dr. Bak Nguyen

0297
FROM PROFESSION HEALTH
"The solution is part of the future, the past holds nothing but pain and sorrow. Even bright, the past will just cast a shadow in the present and future, never a light."
Dr. Bak Nguyen

0298
FROM PROFESSION HEALTH
"Speed, that's the way to cheat time!"
Dr. Bak Nguyen

0299
FROM PROFESSION HEALTH
"Time is the only limited resource. Speed is the only true way to cheat time."
Dr. Bak Nguyen

0300
FROM PROFESSION HEALTH
"From our past, we might find a path to our future."
Dr. Bak Nguyen

0301
FROM INDUSTRIES' DISRUPTORS
"Time is our most precious resource.
Do not waste it in the attachment of past efforts."
Dr. Bak Nguyen

0302
FROM INDUSTRIES' DISRUPTORS
"Time and morale are the most precious resources
for an entrepreneur."
Dr. Bak Nguyen

0303
FROM CHANGING THE WORLD FROM A DENTAL CHAIR
"This is my life! Every moment counts!"
Dr. Bak Nguyen

0304
FROM HYBRID
"Energy is life. We are all alive."
Dr. Bak Nguyen

0305
FROM HYBRID

"You can't destroy energy, but you can distort it. Beware of the consequences."

Dr. Bak Nguyen

0306
FROM HYBRID

"Time is the key, remember, people change."

Dr. Bak Nguyen

0307
FROM HYBRID

"The path is as long traveling to the past than travelling to the future. The choice is yours."

Dr. Bak Nguyen

0308
FROM REBOOT, TO GROW FROM MIDLIFE CRISIS

"Time is the Flow of Life."

Dr. Bak Nguyen

0309
FROM REBOOT, TO GROW FROM MIDLIFE CRISIS

"The Flow of Life is peaceful and powerful."

Dr. Bak Nguyen

0310
FROM REBOOT, TO GROW FROM MIDLIFE CRISIS
"At the surface, the Flow of Life is always the most violent."
Dr. Bak Nguyen

0311
FROM REBOOT, TO GROW FROM MIDLIFE CRISIS
"Life is about choices. Mine is to dive in the Depth of the Flow so I won't have to deal with all the smaller choices."
Dr. Bak Nguyen

0312
FROM FORCES OF NATURE
"Grace and gratitude are the best and my only ways to look at the past and to keep something good from it."
Dr. Bak Nguyen

0313
FROM FORCES OF NATURE
"Once I kissed her lips, the ambition was on and that fire is hard to extinguish."
Dr. Bak Nguyen

0314
FROM FORCES OF NATURE
"No one can escape time. no one can really master time. one can only leverage time."
Dr. Bak Nguyen

0315
FROM THE BOOK OF LEGENDS, VOLUME 1
"Time is like water, it is all around and so easily wasted."
Dr. Bak Nguyen

0316
FROM THE BOOK OF LEGENDS, VOLUME 1
"Have I told you that I do not wait? I have a distorted notion of time to be more precise."
Dr. Bak Nguyen

0317
FROM THE BOOK OF LEGENDS, VOLUME 1
"I hate to wait. There is no hope for me there. I can prepare though."
Dr. Bak Nguyen

0318
FROM SELFMADE
"Our opinion of the past is called experience."
Dr. Bak Nguyen

0319
FROM SELFMADE
"Our opinion of the future is called a dream, a hope. And I am all about hope."
Dr. Bak Nguyen

0320
FROM SELFMADE
"Writing books and telling my story have a similar effect, the danger is to be trapped in the past."
Dr. Bak Nguyen

0321
FROM CHAMPION MINDSET
"To leverage your past into your future."
Dr. Bak Nguyen

0322
FROM CHAMPION MINDSET
"Knowledge is about the past, about facts that can be reproduced and verified. We, our victory lays in the future."
Dr. Bak Nguyen

0323
FROM KRYPTO
"Health is time. Joy is a way to cheat time."
Dr. Bak Nguyen

0324
FROM KRYPTO
"The golden age is about faith and hope. Not summaries and death."
Dr. Bak Nguyen

0325
FROM BRANDING
"To live is the present, to evolve is the future. There is simply nothing else useful."
Dr. Bak Nguyen

0326
FROM HORIZON VOLUME ONE
"Time is the asset that we all possess, until we ungratefully waste it."
Dr. Bak Nguyen

0327
FROM HORIZON VOLUME TWO
"Destiny can't be rushed, even if you are in a hurry, things will come in due time."
Dr. Bak Nguyen

0328
FROM HOW TO NOT FAIL AS A DENTIST
"To see the future in the present time opens the doors to wealth and happiness."
Dr. Bak Nguyen

0329
FROM HOW TO NOT FAIL AS A DENTIST
"There are two main asset classes in life: time and money. Never forget the first one."
Dr. Bak Nguyen

0330
FROM HOW TO NOT FAIL AS A DENTIST
"So yes, not everything is about money, but everything is about time!"
Dr. Bak Nguyen

0331
FROM HOW TO WRITE A SUCCESSFUL BUSINESS PLAN
"Share and make the most of the present time…"

Dr. Bak Nguyen

0332
FROM MINDSET ARMORY
"Even if I do not live with the past nor in the past, I move forward with gratitude, the only part of the past that has a future."

Dr. Bak Nguyen

0333
FROM MINDSET ARMORY
"Indulge yourself to borrow time and happiness. Then, before you run out of time, make the dream come true."

Dr. Bak Nguyen

0334
FROM HUMILITY FOR SUCCESS
"When I talk about the future, I am talking for my voice to echo, so I have an easy way to follow."

Dr. Bak Nguyen

0335
FROM MASTERMIND
"There is no life in the past, just death, and souvenirs."
Dr. Bak Nguyen

0336
FROM MASTERMIND
"To live forever or to be forever young, which is best?"
Dr. Bak Nguyen

0337
FROM MASTERMIND
"I respect my history and my past, but I do not average my past with my future."
Dr. Bak Nguyen

0338
FROM MASTERMIND
"Leveraging is to take the past as spare parts and to combine it as an element of the future system."
Dr. Bak Nguyen

0339
FROM THE ENERGY FORMULA
"Time is no ally to a dreamer."
Dr. Bak Nguyen

0340
FROM PLAYBOOK INTRODUCTION VOLUME 2
"Time is the essence of Life, of opportunity."
Dr. Bak Nguyen

0341
FROM PLAYBOOK INTRODUCTION VOLUME 2
"Credit is your way to buy time, tax-free!"
Dr. Bak Nguyen

0342
FROM PLAYBOOK INTRODUCTION VOLUME 2
"Credit is your way to buy time.
The price paid is the interests on the capital."
Dr. Bak Nguyen

0343
FROM PLAYBOOK INTRODUCTION VOLUME 2
"A debt is the best reminder of your most precious resource, TIME."
Dr. Bak Nguyen

0344
FROM SUCCESS IS A CHOICE
"Time is like the wind. To fight it is not productive.
To have it in our back, well we have
the power of the Universe."
Dr. Bak Nguyen

0345
FROM SUCCESS IS A CHOICE
"Whomever lives in the past is doomed to become a ghost. "
Dr. Bak Nguyen

0346
FROM 90 DAYS CHALLENGE
"It is truly amazing how one can change the perception of time and effort as he keeps his mind busy."
Dr. Bak Nguyen

0347
FROM RISING
"Leverage your time by saving yourself from procrastination."
Dr. Bak Nguyen

0348
FROM RISING
"If you look at the future, you should feel excitement or fear, not security."
Dr. Bak Nguyen

0349
FROM RELEVANCY
"We were left with all of our abilities
and one great gift: TIME!"
Dr. Bak Nguyen

0350
FROM THE BOOK OF LEGENDS VOLUME 3
"Time is the essence of everything worthwhile."
Dr. Bak Nguyen

0351
FROM MIRRORS
"Just like anything else in the universe,
time has its rules and rules can be bent!"
Dr. Bak Nguyen

0352
FROM MIRRORS
"We need to faster the urge in between the meals.
So we created time."
Dr. Bak Nguyen

0353
FROM SHORTCUT VOLUME 1 - HEALING

"Knowing is in from past tense. Feeling is in present tense."

Dr. Bak Nguyen

This is **Shortcut volume 6, POWER**. Welcome to the Alphas.

PART 7
"ABUNDANCE"
by Dr. BAK NGUYEN

Abundance, what is abundance? Is it a destination? Is it a power? Is abundance ultimate happiness? Well, I will start with one crucial statement:

> "More is not Abundance."
> Dr. Bak Nguyen

That's quote #2513. In many of my books, I said that I want more and more, that I do more and more, and that I'll be more and more... Well, I thought that more was **Abundance**, not necessarily.

Wanting more and doing more, I grew and found new powers, almost at each new adventure. My energy and resources were renewed every time that I passed a checkpoint (win). To better understand the checkpoints, I will refer you to my 74th book, **TIMING, TIME MANAGEMENT ON STEROIDS** where I described the **GAMER THEORY**.

In short, the gamer theory stipulates that as you are moving forward, more resources will be provided every time that you cross a checkpoint, just like in the arcade.

Combine the **GAMER THEORY** with my **SPEED** and you can have an idea of the **MOMENTUM** and **ABUNDANCE** that I was swimming in. I grew much, found more and more powers, influences and opportunities. I found those because I ceased **going for carrots**, I now aim at **elephants** instead (reference to **LEADERSHIP, PANDORA'S BOX**).

I thought that Abundance will be the answer to all of our needs, desires, and pains. Until I woke up on a great study.

In the '50s, ethologist Dr. John Calhou conducted an experiment with mice to study the patterns of social behaviours as its population grew. His works spanned from the '50s to the '70s. Basically, Dr. Calhou built a **mice Utopia** with an abundance of food, water, and shelter spaces.

Then, he inserted a small group of mice in the utopia habitat. After an initial settling stage of 100 days, the mice population started to grow to double every 60 days. The **mice Utopia** had a maximum capacity of 3000 mice.

In the **mice Utopia**, predators and most illnesses have been eliminated. Food, water, and shelter were always in abundant supply and accessible from everywhere within the Utopia.

Well, as the population of mice kept doubling every 60 days, the distribution of resources was not equal. As the mice population grew around 2000 individuals, the growth started to plateau.

Aggressivity was more and more present in the population, the mice fighting and biting off each other's tails. At some point, the majority of the subjects had bitting marks and scars on their bodies.

The females slowly grew more and more aggressive and were less available to copulate. Even if food and water were abundant, the females carried fewer and fewer babies. Those who carried on with their pregnancies often abandoned their babies.

There was also the apparition of a special kind of mice. Dr. Calhou named them, the **beautiful mice**: beautiful individuals protected by others, who mainly spent their days grooming, eating, and sleeping. They were beautiful and peaceful individuals, but they had no inclination to reproduce or copulate.

If put together with the crowd of mice, the beautiful mice are just lost and have a very difficult time adapting and showing any social skills. Beautiful but very stupid!

As the population crowded the Utopia, plateauing in the 2000s, violence became more and more predominant. Some individuals became repeated targets of attacks.

Between violence, the less available females, and the apparition of the **beautiful mice** generation, the population started to decline. It peaks around 2200 mice and when straight done until all mice eventually died. Dr. Calhou repeated the same experience, again and again, always resulting with the same trends and outcomes.

Well, I will not interpret the results of that model of society and social behaviours. Instead, it opened my eyes to the undeniable fact: Abundance was not the solution.

"Growth happens at the giving end."
Dr. Bak Nguyen

Until that point, I was sure that **Abundance** was the answer to everything, to happiness. Well, with Dr. Calhou's research, I saw Abundance for what it really is: a power. One that, if yield correctly will empower much growth. For that, you must be at the giving end of the equation, providing Abundance.

On the other end, if you are the one receiving and eating Abundance, it will corrupt and burn most of your senses and body until complete annihilation.

"Abundance is a drug and its addiction is without mercy!"
Dr. Bak Nguyen

That's quote #2514. I started this journey telling you that this volume, the 6th volume of the **SHORTCUT** franchise, **POWER** is the darkest of the series, well, even **ABUNDANCE** can turn and burn us alive.

Throughout my journeys, the themes of **SHARING** to grow and **SERVICING** others to reduce friction and resistance were dominant. I wrote what I know and what I feel. I wrote from my instincts.

Even the inclusion of **ABUNDANCE** within this journey was a mystery to me. Something in me pushed for its inclusion. Until I read Dr. Calhou, I did not understand my own logic and instincts. Now, it is all too clear.

> "Abundance is a power. Yield it to provide and you are powerful. Stop and stare and it will eat you up alive from the inside out…"
> Dr. Bak Nguyen

That's quote #2515. That said, Abundance is amongst the most charismatic goal but don't be fool by its perfumes, charms, and pleasure. Instead, yield it to provide to others and, for a time, you will have shared with more ease.

I found **Abundance** looking for more. My salvation was that I was looking to do more, to live more, to be more! I did not get bigger by eating but by sharing. That is how my momentum grew with the support of Abundance.

And since I am growing on the **bed of Abundance**, I now have more resources to do more, to try more, to be more! But I know that the day that I will lose my **SPEED** and my desire to serve, that day, if I keep *sleeping* with **Abundance**, that day, what loved and empowered me will start poisoning my veins and minds. That will be the end.

But until then, with **Time** and **Abundance** by my side, I am discovering the Universe, serving the world.

This is **Shortcut volume 6, POWER**. Welcome to the Alphas.

> Hammering air three times over
> and it will become steel.
>
> Dr. BAK NGUYEN

PART 8
"52 ABUNDANCE QUOTES"
by Dr. BAK NGUYEN

1448
FROM SYMPHONY OF SKILLS
"Life starts when we start giving."
Dr. Bak Nguyen

1449
FROM LEADERSHIP, PANDORA'S BOX
"The taste of abundance demands that one gives up the carrot!"
Dr. Bak Nguyen

1450
FROM LEADERSHIP, PANDORA'S BOX
"Life is abundant, and we can taste all of it together."
Dr. Bak Nguyen

1451
FROM LEADERSHIP, PANDORA'S BOX
"We don't have generosity, and we are generosity."
Dr. Bak Nguyen

1452
FROM LEADERSHIP, PANDORA'S BOX
"Be generous, and you will be limitless. Generous, not stupid!"
Dr. Bak Nguyen

1453
FROM LEADERSHIP, PANDORA'S BOX
"The Universe is always expanding, so should our minds and hearts."

Dr. Bak Nguyen

1454
FROM IDENTITY, ANTHOLOGY OF QUESTS
"Abundance is blessed by the creativity of those with vision, with curiosity, with ambition."

Dr. Bak Nguyen

1455
FROM IDENTITY, ANTHOLOGY OF QUESTS
"Music is emotion. In other words, free style history."

Dr. Bak Nguyen

1456
FROM IDENTITY, ANTHOLOGY OF QUESTS
"Abundance can be reached but nothing is free!"

Dr. Bak Nguyen

1457
FROM IDENTITY, ANTHOLOGY OF QUESTS
"Three is the beginning of abundance or the end of one."

Dr. Bak Nguyen

1458
FROM IDENTITY, ANTHOLOGY OF QUESTS
"Connecting is the way to abundance! Remember that!"
Dr. Bak Nguyen

1459
FROM IDENTITY, ANTHOLOGY OF QUESTS
"Abundance is bliss, the math does not have to be half as complex since we just need to know how to add up and to multiply!"
Dr. Bak Nguyen

1460
FROM INDUSTRIES' DISRUPTORS
"Be open, be kind, don't wait and do not get attached. By being respectful and generous, you will attract those you seek. You only need to sort out the others."
Dr. Bak Nguyen

1461
FROM CHANGING THE WORLD FROM A DENTAL CHAIR
"It's possible to have it all!"
Dr. Bak Nguyen

1462
FROM THE POWER BEHIND THE ALPHA
"Gratitude, gratitude. If Confidence is sexy, Gratitude is addictive."
Dr. Bak Nguyen

1463
FROM THE POWER BEHIND THE ALPHA
"The next phase after humility is generosity."
Dr. Bak Nguyen

1464
FROM THE POWER BEHIND THE ALPHA
"You can have it all, only if you ask for it and that you are ready to receive!"
Dr. Bak Nguyen

1465
FROM HYBRID
"Creativity x Kindness = Abundance"
Dr. Bak Nguyen

1466
FROM REBOOT, TO GROW FROM MIDLIFE CRISIS
"Abundance does not come from one, it is defined by the multitude and by freedom."
Dr. Bak Nguyen

1466
FROM FORCES OF NATURE
"Life is about happiness.
And happiness is about worth!"
Dr. Bak Nguyen

1467
FROM FORCES OF NATURE
"Generosity is the answer to face Abundance."
Dr. Bak Nguyen

1468
FROM FORCES OF NATURE
"Abundance and Generosity allowed me
to put an end to having to choose."
Dr. Bak Nguyen

1469
FROM CHAMPION MINDSET
"Be respectful to welcome the possibilities; be grateful to keep the abundance of life within reach."
Dr. Bak Nguyen

1470
FROM BRANDING
"YES it is possible, YES is powerful,
YES there is hope."
Dr. Bak Nguyen

1471
FROM HORIZON VOLUME ONE
"I am rich thanks to my souvenirs and
the way I keep playing them over time."
Dr. Bak Nguyen

1472
FROM HORIZON VOLUME ONE
"To keep one's heart open to the opportunities
is the only key to happiness and abundance."
Dr. Bak Nguyen

1473
FROM HORIZON VOLUME ONE
"Embrace yourselves, embrace love, embrace Life.
Only when you open up that the colours
and the savours can get intense!"
Dr. Bak Nguyen

1474
FROM HORIZON VOLUME TWO
"We are free to choose to have it all.
Not all at once, but we can have it all
if we prioritize and keep focus. "
Dr. Bak Nguyen

1475
FROM MASTERMIND
"Abundance of Time, of opportunities,
of energy, of resources."
Dr. Bak Nguyen

1476
FROM THE ENERGY FORMULA
"Abundance is not about having or being.
It is about mattering."
Dr. Bak Nguyen

1477
FROM THE ENERGY FORMULA
"To embrace Abundance, one has to give up fear."
Dr. Bak Nguyen

1478
FROM AMONGST THE ALPHAS, VOLUME 2
"The more you'll give, the more you'll grow!
That's the equation of Abundance!"
Dr. Bak Nguyen

1479
FROM SUCCESS IS A CHOICE
"The magic of life is to to reduce but to multiple.
Stop amputating and start expanding."
Dr. Bak Nguyen

1480
FROM SUCCESS IS A CHOICE
"Time is a commodity. Abundance is about time.
That's how everyone can taste it,
we only need to know how."
Dr. Bak Nguyen

1481
FROM RISING
"From hope and abundance, I gave the public
what they wanted, hope for abundance."
Dr. Bak Nguyen

1482
FROM RISING
"Actually, we are either stuck in scarcity
or ungrateful about our abundance."
Dr. Bak Nguyen

1483
FROM RISING
"The true POWER OF ABUNDANCE isn't in what you enjoy today, but what you can bring to the table tomorrow!"
Dr. Bak Nguyen

1484
FROM RISING
"The first premise to the LAW OF ABUNDANCE is to master the POWER OF GRATITUDE."
Dr. Bak Nguyen

1485
FROM RISING
"Embrace the new and be flexible to merge with the new. Soon enough, you'll be shaping the future, from and with ABUNDANCE."
Dr. Bak Nguyen

1486
FROM RISING
"A multitude of beginnings to eclipse the ends, start more than you end to stay in ABUNDANCE."
Dr. Bak Nguyen

1487
FROM AFTERMATH
"Philanthropy is not just your shield,
but also your best leverage."
Dr. Bak Nguyen

1488
FROM AFTERMATH
"Philanthropy is not charity."
Dr. Bak Nguyen

1489
FROM MIDAS TOUCH
"Embrace the vastness, the possibilities
and enjoy your new found freedom!"
Dr. Bak Nguyen

1490
FROM MIDAS TOUCH
"Kindness attracts kindness, success attracts success,
everything started with attraction… and attraction
only works when one opens up."
Dr. Bak Nguyen

1491
FROM TORNADO
"Scarcity and Abundance, when nature permits, come down to a state of mind."
Dr. Bak Nguyen

1492
FROM EMPOWERMENT
"I wanted it all. I got it all because I embraced abundance, flexibility and gave up perfection and exclusivity."
Dr. Bak Nguyen

1493
FROM THE UAX STORY
"Abundance, Success and Happiness, all in one word: Sharing."
Dr. Bak Nguyen

1494
FROM 1SELF
"And we exchange freedom for security."
Dr. Bak Nguyen

1495
FROM ALPHA LADDERS VOLUME 2
"To be rich is to have more.
Not more than the person next door. Just more."
Dr. Bak Nguyen

1496
FROM THE BOOK OF LEGENDS VOLUME 3
"Abundance is to create more than we need and to react to such quantity."
Dr. Bak Nguyen

1497
FROM MIRRORS
"Life is abundance and multitude, not single.
So all shall be."
Dr. Bak Nguyen

1498
FROM MIRRORS
"Once life was abundant between birth and death.
We made it scarce drawing lines as past and future."
Dr. Bak Nguyen

1499

FROM SHORTCUT VOLUME 1 - HEALING

"At 8, the possibilities and the energy seem to be infinite."

Dr. Bak Nguyen

This is **Shortcut volume 6, POWER**. Welcome to the Alphas.

Hammering air three times over
and it will become steel.

Dr. BAK NGUYEN

PART 9
"THE POWER OF QUOTES"
by Dr. BAK NGUYEN

Have you found your powers yet? Even if you haven't, now you feel them erupting and storming inside of you. You still need to grow enough to become their vessels. And this is what we are, a vessel to express the **Forces of Nature**.

If we understand what is power, we will grow strong enough to vibrate at its frequency and to become one with the power. That is finding your talents. In the Chicken books series, the words I found to explain it to William were: "A chicken needs to open its mind to grow into a **lion heart**."

Then, to master and yield that talent, you need to put it into good use, serving others. In **chicken books' terms**, it was: "Then, a **lion heart**, if it keeps its heart open, will grow into a **dragon heart**. And the dragon can fly."

And what's next? Well, in the first chicken trilogy, William, 8 at that time, asked me: "Papa, if the dragons are real, why have I never seen one?" And that took me by surprise. I have no idea what to answer… fortunately, I am a fast thinker.

My answer to my child was cute and clever: "It is because the dragon change shape. You see William, once a dragon masters a power (emotion), it takes the shape of that power.

Then, to keep the fun going, after yielding the power, the dragon will forget it and go on to learn a new power, taking, eventually a new form. So, look around, there are dragons everywhere, you only don't know what to look for."

That was the best answer a dad could give his kid to complete the story and the last tome of the **chicken trilogy**, that was cute. And then, I went on to write the story with William. I needed to find inspiration from real-life events to have a narrative that would make sense and be appealing. And that's how it became clever.

A simple storyline, from a **chicken heart** into a **lion heart** and from a lion heart into a **dragon heart**; from opening up your mind to opening up your heart and to keep going, not stalling neither on the medals nor the past to keep the fun flowing:

> "I just gave William the secret to find,
> not only power but the abundance of powers."
> Dr. Bak Nguyen

That's quote #2516. So if you wonder what is the power of a quote, well, my entire library is the result of the combining of different quotes bridging from one step to the next. The trilogy of the chicken brought it to its essence, having me to explain secrets of life to an 8 years old and using his words to write.

From one bridge to the next, we found the secret together. I knew about the chicken heart and the lion heart story. The dragon, that was from his questions… and we discovered a great **Path to Abundance** together, as father and son.

> "Hammering air three times over
> and it will become steel."
> Dr. Bak Nguyen

Three times, one trilogy, and the secret to Abundance. Can it be a better example? One quote at a time, one bridge at a time. One win after the next, keep moving, light and open, and you will find more and more powers to try, to yield, to become one with.

Now you have the recipe and the map, from quote to quote. Walking this journey, the 6th volume of the

SHORTCUT series, POWER, I took the time to slow down and to look at the ripple effects and the consequence of such discoveries.

In medicine, the first golden rule is not to cause harm. The second golden rule is to get consent, informed consent. This is me honouring the art and science I've been given as a doctor. This is your informed consent.

Before running to your powers and riding them, know that powers are not serving you, they are serving the Universe. You are just the vessel, for a given time, to express that will and power. You do not possess power, at your best, you may become one with power… for a while.

And that's what you need to understand yielding power. Next come the classic, 8 of the 77 famous quotes to bridge you to your powers.

> "A quote at a time, a win after the next."
> Dr. Bak Nguyen

That's quote #2517.

FAMOUS QUOTE 1

0020
FROM MOMENTUM TRANSFER
"Control with wisdom is called influence."
Dr. Bak Nguyen

I wrote that one as I was finding ways to bridge **physical momentum** into **mental momentum** and vice versa. To do so, I needed a way to canalize the energy generated and use it as a boost to make the transfer.

From one realm to the next, the only way to succeed such transition was to reduce the friction to its smallest denominator. It became clear that to stand the ground and to knock down the walls were not the ways to achieve the transfer of energy.

You don't believe me? Let's cover that for a minute. I am in momentum and all pumped up with hormones and adrenaline after an instance training session, I am ready to tackle anything. Then, you give me an opponent obstructing my way. If the opponent is much bigger than me (wall), I will run into him with all the energy that I have accumulated and as we hit, I will transfer that power to the shock, to him.

Best case scenario, I will have knocked him down. And then, the shock will have taken away most of the available energy and I will be left with little. I still have to pick up the pieces, his and mine. All actions have consequences. That's not momentum!

In the more plausible scenario, we will both be knocked down by the blast and will fall on our asses. The energy went to fuel anger and aggressivity on both parties.

But now, the fight, I am stuck fighting with my energy. This is not even momentum, it is even worse as I now have to produce the energy to fuel the fight. And, if I survive, it will be to pick up the pieces. That's not momentum, that's power burning you!

And what happens in the case of me running into a small wall, one that I will just run over without blinking? Well, I will have stained with blood my trail. Other than the regret and the ripple effect in which I am awakening the **raise of my rival**, the one that will eventually destroy me.

This is how the powers and the Universe work, balancing and contra-balancing. These are all resistance that I do not need.

To skip such waste and drama, I found a better way, once with much less frictions and with little contra-balance. I empower instead of fighting. As I empower, I am helping someone else. With all of my energy, as I am sharing and as the other party is connecting, the energy grew and we both can feel it. That's already more energy available with little cost.

That was just step one. Then, if synergy is reached, the energy increase exponentially, being much greater than the sum of the energy we both pitch in. To me, that's great leverage and **insane return**.

The beauty about energy is that you do not need to divide it, both have access to the synergy without taking away anything from the other party. That's energy. If we were not focused on energy but on power, that's another story, one we all know the conclusion to…

So to me, I got in that synergy with a boost from a previous momentum. It can be physical or mental, the hormones are the same. I leveraged that. Then I put it all in, empowering and helping someone I can get along with. Then, the energy has a chance to grow exponentially.

If that person is not one with whom I can create synergy, that's fine too, since I will still have twice the energy (the sum of his and mine) available to keep moving forward and not taking anything away from that person (except if that person falls into jealousy, in that case, he will be poisoning his heart with hate, but that was not me, it was all him or her).

If I move quickly enough, I even have a chance to outpace jealousy. So once again, speed is my remedy.

In the eventuality that we found synergy, we will both be in ecstasy and in abundance of energy for a while. Well, I will use that new and bigger momentum as the boost to go even further, faster and higher, repeating the same experience with new and more people.

All of that was possible because I was in control. I knew how to handle power and let it express its way without corrupting my veins: I served and empowered. Then, I leveraged quickly the increase of energy available to help and empower more and more.

I was in control, not of power, but of myself to make it work. My powers even change shape, from power to influence for me to keep growing and advancing quickly without much friction. Eventually, I became one with certain powers. The next step for me is to let someone yield me...

Speed is the remedy. Speed and power can only do as much as the resistance they have to overcome. Remove the resistance and the growth is exponential. I started with sharing and with empowering, which took care of much of the resistance. Much but not all of it.

Then, to keep moving forward, I learnt to let go of my anchors, one after the next. I got rid of as much attachments as possible. I face even less resistance. Then, I needed more, more energy, more speed, more results. The last piece of resistance was myself, my identity, and my values. That too, I put on the table and leverage accordingly to grow my momentum and to become one with my powers.

For those intrigued, I will encourage you to look for **THE ENERGY FORMULA**, my 53rd book. Control, wisdom, and influence, that's how I became one with power, one with the universe.

FAMOUS QUOTE 2

0027
FROM LEVERAGE COMMUNICATION INTO SUCCESS
"Humility is not the denial of oneself but the acceptance of one true nature."

Dr. Bak Nguyen

Before one can find and yield power. One needs to be ready. We are the **vessels** of the **Forces of Nature**, not their masters. The cool part is that the Universe is so large that it does not always care about how its energy (forces) is expressed. And this is where we can make a difference.

The way the universe works is that it will release its forces and will contra-balance to course-correct. That is the law of the universe, one that none of us can change. We can only learn about it and try to avoid the **contra-balance**. And that is within the ripple effect of our own actions, as little as they might be.

But before one can yield and become power, even before one can discover power, one needs to be ready first. And being ready starts with the acknowledgement and the awareness of who and what we are. This is the key to our awakening.

One might feel the power storming inside but for as long as one did not acknowledge who he or she is, that is just a storm, not an empowerment. Each of us has a part of the divine, of the universe beating in us, that is what gives us life.

The next level of expression of that life force is through our talents. You must be humble enough to accept and to acknowledge them. That's not bragging, that's gratitude!

Then, with the talents received, you need to express them. The only way I found to express mine without too much negative ripple effect, was to put my talents in the service of others. Doing so, they are putting their energy and resources with mine to achieve our common goal.

For as long as I was the one providing, I grew, more and more, with nothing but good ripple effects. That took care of most of the resistance, but jealousy. And jealousy, that ate and chewed on my bones for decades, it did because I loved and stick around waiting for those I loved. Well, it took me half of my life to see what jealousy really is and how it can turn love into hate.

I was fortunate to escape from that with meat on my bones. I had the wisdom to not carry that hate and pain with me either. So I keep empowering and helping, but now, without attachment nor expectation. With those gone, I and now less vulnerable and more available.

Don't get me wrong, I still love with all of my heart. I love, hope for the best, and try to keep my expectations down, for the sake of all parties. That's how I raised my son to become my buddy, my best buddy!

For the rest of jealousy, I act with power and momentum and I move on with speed, with ease. The longer I will stay, the more the danger of jealousy showing up with its ugly head.

> "And don't be mistaken, jealousy will always show up, that's the contra-balance to success."
> **Dr. Bak Nguyen**

That's quote #2518. So the first step to empowerment is through **acknowledgement** and **awareness**. Those are **humility** and **gratitude**, not arrogance. Even for the believers, what do you think that God will think of you if you ignore the gifts he prepared for you? I cannot think of anything more arrogant and ungrateful.

Then, as you have to deliver on these talents, you'll need confidence to express the power within. Once more, you are a vessel, not power. Those who will call you arrogant are those threatened by the power that you are expressing.

For as long as you were serving, keep your eyes on the goal and let the fearful and jealous whisper behind. That's **confidence** growing from **humility**. And yes, confidence and humility do co-exist, they even empower one another.

And then, I told you to move forward before jealousy has the time to show its ugly head. Well, to do that, jump to your next cause, to the next people to empower. In modern terms, this is called branding and communication.

Well, those are not bragging but effective communication. You need to attract those you help to you, not going to them. Can you think of a better way to keep momentum?

For as long as you keep in movement, humility, confidence, empowerment, and communication will keep you ahead.

FAMOUS QUOTE 3

0029
FROM THE BOOK OF LEGENDS, VOLUME 1
*"To have an open mind is step one.
To keep growing, one needs an open heart."*
Dr. Bak Nguyen

By now, this should be something obvious to each of you. To open our minds means to acknowledge and to be aware. First of who and what we are, then of our surroundings. That is how we are discovering our powers.

To train and grow your powers, you need to put them to good use. To do that without contra-balance and resistance at your first strokes, you need to put your powers to the service of others and this is the open heart phase.

As I told you earlier, I knew that and as my son wanted to write books with me, I leverage the opportunity to teach him to open his mind and heart. We created the chicken books franchise together.

Writing with William, gave me the opportunity to filter my thoughts and wording to appeal to a child. In other, I sorted out my ideas to keep only their purest essence. We started with opening our minds to open our hearts… and then, to keep moving forward with fun and lightness (the Dragon Heart story).

Well, I was open to write with my son because I am a man of my word. I had no clue how to write a book with a kid of 8 years old. I spent a whole year with that in the back of my mind. I even threw away a 1/3 of a movie script that I was working on with William. I kept my mind open. Finally, the answer was right there, in front of me, the whole time, as William picked up my iPhone and talked to Siri!

I have my mind open, the heart was his. William kept sharing because he wanted to connect with me, deeply, genuinely. By that time, I faced family's storms, one after the next, and have a very bumpy ride with Tranie. William stepped in to canalize my energy and to help me refocus. That's how our story started rising as father and son.

Then, we reacted to one another, empowering each other and we reached synergy within days, days! How do you think that we wrote 8 books within a month, with illustrations and editing? We were flowing in synergy!

I kept my mind open and empower him to open his. He offered his heart and it saved mine. Then, we had so much energy available that even after 8 books and 2 world records, he wanted more! We went on to write 22 chicken books together within the following months.

FAMOUS QUOTE 4

0042
FROM BRANDING
"I kept the "Dr." on to remind me to
always put your interests before mine."
Dr. Bak Nguyen

Even if I am the one writing and teaching you about powers and the map to powers, I am not above the traps and downfalls myself. I also try to walk what I preach, so Gratitude above all.

This is the context of keeping the Dr. in front of my name, even when I am not the attending doctor. I did so to honour the sacrifices of my parents and the trust Society put in me as it accepted me as a member of the medical elite.

You know my story. I became a doctor to honour my parents and their sacrifices. I am much more of a sensitive soul and an artist than a surgeon. That said, I became a successful and loved surgeon, one with an international reputation. I succeed as such, not because I was the best surgeon but because I was the most human, looking to connect and treat people first, not their teeth nor their illness.

I became loved and respected because people felt that I care and that I will not walk away until it is done. Always, my profession taught me to always put the interest of my patients before mine.

Now, as I am entering a whole new realm, one of power and influence, I am doing it with the same core values, putting the interest of those under my care before mine. In an operation room, that has been hammered in my core but on the field of power, it is so easy to lose track and to focus on our belly button. And we know what will happen as the focus closes down on us, resistance will grow and the power we bear will burn the bearer.

So I found a quick fix to that, leveraging my past and gratitude, keeping the Dr. in front of my name. Every time that I am hearing my name, the first sound before my name is to remind me that I am here for that person first. The name following is with what I will be empowering and helping.

That was genuinely the fix and patch that I found to avoid burning myself from the powers that I currently carry. Branding myself Dr. Bak, the stretch was not a big one from my previous appellation, Dr. Nguyen. The main difference is that Dr. Nguyen is a product of society while Dr. Bak is a reaction to the same society.

Indeed, Nguyen is one of the most common names for an Asian of Vietnamese descend, left alone an Asian doctor. My parents are Vietnamese, I am Canadian! Not just by status but from the inside out. During my Quest of Identity, I even went back to the country of my ancestors, only to feel how different I was, while for the first time in my life, I have the right skin colour to fit in. I was standing out as a stranger!

So the name is common and one that was given to me. I did not have a say in that one. Then, the title of Dr. that I received after surviving the selection process and all of the requirements, that was a gift from Society, I joined the ranks of the medical elite. Actually, I was trained and ready to serve.

More than 15 years later, I woke up and found my true calling. I kept the Dr. title, not to brag but as a homage to the past and one looking to the future with a plan, to empower, to share, and to grow. Bak, is the name my friends gave me, from the contraction of Ba-Khoa, my given name. Bak is the name I built with and built on.

So today, Dr. Bak is both available and coming to you with a promise, the nobility of a doctor in medical sciences. But that became also a great branding exercise as people discovered me. They loved the promise of the Dr. and the familiarity of Bak, as a first name, as someone close and accessible.

That is how I grew from being a dentist to a world anchor people know as the host of the Alphas. I am Dr. Bak, what can I do for you?

I am not saying that I can help everyone and will surely not impose myself where I cannot find an angle to make a difference. But my promise is that I will be listening first.

Dr. Bak's rise is barely beginning. If Time and Health allow, I will keep sharing my journey with you in future books, documentaries, and conferences! Welcome to the Alphas.

FAMOUS QUOTE 5

0052
FROM HUMILITY FOR SUCCESS
"Until it is done, it is air, good air but only air."
Dr. Bak Nguyen

This is the gift and the curse of all the visionaries. An idea is air and the strength of a visionary is not only to see and to link what is not, yet but also to keep moving forward with what he or she has in hand, air.

On the way, opinions will tear the visionary down. They will try their best. The most common and hurtful is that these opinions will come from those he or she loved the most and held close to his or her heart. To survive doubt and separation is the strength of the visionary. To heal from these wounds is the journey of each visionary.

And then what? And then, we push forward, walking the map in our mind and heart that nobody else sees. No need to tell you how Doubt will greatly handicap the walker. A tread of doubt might throw the journey off course.

To protect yourself from that, your only shot is to bet everything on your Confidence. This is not blind trust. You see your vision clearly, you just need the confidence to walk the path until it is done. For that you need to feel, that is how you will communicate your vision from your mind to your body.

Then, people will see what you saw and praise you. As it becomes a safe way to them, to you, it is now boring.

Your power was curiosity and the taste for adventure. You had superpowers then, walking the thin air and the unknown. If you stay still in the know, your own powers will burn you inside out. That is why you will eventually leave and walk thin air, yet again.

As a seasoned visionary, walking thin air is no novelty to me. I wrote that quote only to reassure those amongst us who are walking the path for the first time. Those who doubt will be targeted and broken. We've all been there, alone and isolated.

Well, this is a voice from the universe, contra-balancing that doubt. You are walking on thin air, keep going before doubt fogs the clarity and you got lost in your own vision. I don't know you, I don't know your vision, therefore, I am not judging you. But that heart of yours, I know and understand its feeling and what it needs to keep pushing: the reassurance that you are doing great!

And yet, believing is not enough, one still has to walk that path and enlighten the world with his or her new discovery. Those doubting before will soon turn into followers soon. Out of the trade, you are showing them the path, they will leverage on your vision and curiosity. But out of the equation, both parties feed your confidence, yours and yours alone!

> "Growth happens at the giving end."
> Dr. Bak Nguyen

And this is how you will keep growing if you did not fall victim to doubt on the way. And humility? Be careful not to fall into the trap of being humble: one should listen.

You are humble to recognize who you are and what you received. On your vision, if it is new, no one knows the way. You alone might have a chance with your map and clarity. That is for the direction to walk toward to.

About the walk, be open and humble to learn from others who know how to walk on thin air to ease your journey. You know where to go but you don't have to reinvent the wheel on how to get there. Just get there as soon as possible!

FAMOUS QUOTE 6

0057
FROM AMONGST THE ALPHAS, VOLUME 2
"Be bold, confident, and humble."
Dr. Bak Nguyen

Once more, this is addressing the visionaries. Be bold first because you need to convince yourself of where to go and why you are walking that path. By being bold, you are boosting confidence just like a diver will take a deep breath before the dive.

Be confident as you are diving in the depth. Even with that boost of confidence, your air is running thin and low. Doubting and indecision will consume much of that precious air and either you will have to go back or, as you keep pushing forward, that will greatly reduce your chance of success.

On thin air, your only chance is to surf as fast as possible to reach the **checkpoint**. The bolder you were, the more confidence in reserve you have in your tank.

The more confidence you have, the longer you can go... how far can one go with that tank of confidence, speed will be the decisive factor.

> "And Speed is a derivative of Confidence.
> Without confidence, there is no speed."
> **Dr. Bak Nguyen**

That's quote #2519. And what about being humble? Well, as I said earlier, you know the path, you have the clarity of your vision. Even if you know where to go, you can ease your way learning from people who travelled ways similar to yours.

I never said to ask them for their opinions. I said to learn about how they made it through their journey, and find inspiration to walk yours. In real life, those are mentors that you will meet on the way. The question to raise is never: "What do you think of...?" Rather, "How would you ...?"

The biggest danger that any visionary faces, is to shield him or herself up and to blind their own Confidence thinking that they are right and have all the answers. That will be your doom walking the path of the visionary!

Be bold to know what is your vision.
Be wise enough to see the difference
Between an opinion and an experience

Be humble to ease your way
From the experience of mentors.

FAMOUS QUOTE 7

0069
FROM TORNADO
"Dream and the means will come."
Dr. Bak Nguyen

This is the mindset that I first used as I was finding out about the **power of speed** and the **power of momentum**. Do not confuse the 2. As the power of speed is to go fast to beat jealousy and resistance, the power of momentum is to do bigger and bolder things with ease.

When we talk about dreams and resources, we are talking about momentum. That said, once the right mindset is in place, speed will explode and propel everything skyrocketing to new heights. But let's go back to the beginning of this quote.

To dream is to see without boundaries.
To dream is to acknowledge our desires
Without any but or if.

To dream is to allow ourself
A moment of truth to be bold,
To feel whole.

In other words, to dream is to see clearly. What do you think a vision is? To see clearly! So everything starts with a dream. The more vivid is the dream, the more clarity one will have. And what does that means in everyday life?

Well, as you dream, you feel elevated. Keep that feeling close to your heart and leverage on it to push your body to walk the dream until that feeling will come from touching instead of projecting. On the way, the hormones that your body is producing, that's not air, that's all true!

The dream may be thin air but not the walk. As soon as you are walking, you are materializing the emotions and sensations you felt as you were dreaming. The souvenir of those feelings will push you to create trails that will lead to your dream.

Touch the finished line and you have both the trails and the destination to greatness. If not greatness, at least novelty. And that is what you are leaving behind for others to find and to discover. What they will walk, feel, experience is your past. But as they are travelling it, their resources (part of it) will be yours, for a little time.

This is a great example of the checkpoints and gamer mentality. But first, you have to cross the finished line. Until that point, you were running on the energy of your vision. The only way to gain more energy on the way was to pass these **checkpoints**. So aim for your next checkpoint (win) as soon as possible to refuel and replenish.

Dream and establish a map of checkpoints on your way there. The checkpoints will be the key to your success. The bigger the dream, the more checkpoints you will have on your way.

In other words, dream big and jump from win to win to build up your momentum and confidence. Then, nothing is out of reach.

FAMOUS QUOTE 8

0071
FROM ALPHA LADDERS VOLUME 2
"Growth occurs at the giving end, always."
Dr. Bak Nguyen

I don't think that I need to explain this one at this point. If the concept of sharing to grow appeared very early on my journey writing and sharing with you, the idea that growth occurs at the giving end took shape into words much later as I started structuring the Alphas, internationally.

What is an Alpha you will ask? Here is a speech that I pronounced online in the context of recruiting thinkers and shakers to address our economy after the COVID war:

> What's an Alpha? An Alpha is the first, on the scene, the first one with ideas and visions. I've been asked in an interview once about me and my Alphas. Allow me to straight up the record here: they are not my Alphas, they are Alphas.
>
> My role is just to ease the connection between people, with vision, between people with the drive to make a difference, and people with the need to contribute. Those are Alphas. If you look in the Greek alphabet, Alpha means first. The continuation of this, a first will have to be followed by other people.
>
> Common wisdom will say that a great leader will not gather more followers but he or she will help more leaders to emerge. This is an Alpha. An Alpha is somebody who will

lead by example, trying to provoke the situation and to inspire others to join and to do even better.

By no means we are different, by no means we are special. What is special about us, Alphas? It's our will to make a difference, our will to contribute, and our will to help. Being an Alpha, it's not who we are but who we choose to be. The hope I'm bringing here, is that we are all Alphas. If we chose so.

That is how my son of 10, earned his way to become an Alpha. Yes, he is legacy but trust me, when you're in front of the camera, no matter who your dad is, that will not help you. You need to have something true from your heart and to share it with the rest of the world. It will be for you (at home) to decide if that message was worth your time.

We live in very special times, where all of our values are tested heavily, daily. To inspire the good out of each other, this is what we need more than ever. For this, I urge you to look in the mirror to seek that light, in your eyes, saying that today can be better. You know, that you are an Alpha and we need you.

I am Dr. Bak, I am an Alpha, and so are you.

That was the **Alpha Declaration**. As I defined the Alphas a year after launching the organization, I gained much insights about the **WHY**, the **WHAT**, and the **HOW**.

I was a single man seeking answers and seeking to connect. Then, I went online and connected as the entire world was put on hold at the same time (in the three first months of the COVID war). That was my opportunity and I took it.

As I was connecting with thinkers and drivers, leaders of industries, I attracted them by empowering their perspective about what was going on and how to help everyone to leverage themselves through the trouble times.

Most if not all of the people I hosted on the **Alphashow** and **Alpha Summits** were better qualified and much more knowledgable than I was myself. Yet, I was the anchor because I welcome them in and empowered them to share.

Because I empowered them, they felt good and gave me both, their trust and friendship. And this is what I am always looking for, friendship! Today, the Alphas is an elite group of leaders who are still looking forward to share and to empower the world through this Post-COIVD era.

Well, I gave it my all as I was hosting the Alphas. I gave and I grew. The more I gave (empowered) the more Alphas were happy and joined. They even referred one another. I kept empowering and I grew my network in a matter of days.

I do not hold any power on the Alphas but when I call or when I write, they are always answering. Now, we are networking our knowledge and resources to solve issues that alone, we were scratching our heads on.

What we don't know and seek, another Alphas has already done it in the past! That's the power of connection, once trust and friendship have been established.

I grew because I gave. Well, each of the Alphas joining grew too, as they connected and gave. The more they were open to share, the more connections they will have. And with more connections, they now have more resources to solve their question marks.

Give first and be open to grow!

This is **Shortcut volume 6, POWER**. Welcome to the Alphas.

Dr. BAK NGUYEN

PART 10
"FAMOUS QUOTES"
by Dr. BAK NGUYEN

0001
FROM SYMPHONY OF SKILLS
"The pain of the problem has to be greater than the pain of change."
Dr. Bak Nguyen

0002
FROM SYMPHONY OF SKILLS
"Sharing is the way to grow."
Dr. Bak Nguyen

0003
FROM LEADERSHIP, PANDORA'S BOX
"One's legend can only begin the day one's Quest of Identity is over."
Dr. Bak Nguyen

0004
FROM IDENTITY, ANTHOLOGY OF QUESTS
"Gratitude is the only past with a future."
Dr. Bak Nguyen

0005
FROM PROFESSION HEALTH
"Mine was, forgive yourself."
Dr. Bak Nguyen

0006
FROM INDUSTRIES' DISRUPTORS
"To walk on thin ice is a dangerous game.
To run is safer. To surf is the easiest."
Dr. Bak Nguyen

0007
FROM INDUSTRIES' DISRUPTORS
"If I have changed the world from a dental chair,
you are all in a better position than I am
to change the world."
Dr. Bak Nguyen

0008
FROM INDUSTRIES' DISRUPTORS
"The day you are fighting to raise the average instead
of beating it, that day, you've joined the leadership."
Dr. Bak Nguyen

0009
FROM INDUSTRIES' DISRUPTORS
"At the end of the day, business is communication."
Dr. Bak Nguyen

0010
FROM INDUSTRIES' DISRUPTORS
"Make leverage of each of your liabilities, and you will always be moving forward."
Dr. Bak Nguyen

0011
FROM INDUSTRIES' DISRUPTORS
"I believe in myself and I do it for God, not the other way around."
Dr. Bak Nguyen

0012
FROM INDUSTRIES' DISRUPTORS
"Always choose the path of least resistance."
Dr. Bak Nguyen

0013
FROM INDUSTRIES' DISRUPTORS
"Be mindful of the consequences."
Dr. Bak Nguyen

0014
FROM CHANGING THE WORLD FROM A DENTAL CHAIR
"Hammering air three times over and it will become steel."
Dr. Bak Nguyen

0015
FROM CHANGING THE WORLD FROM A DENTAL CHAIR
"Mdex, for joy for life."
Dr. Bak Nguyen

0016
FROM CHANGING THE WORLD FROM A DENTAL CHAIR
"Confidence is sexy."
Dr. Bak Nguyen

0017
FROM CHANGING THE WORLD FROM A DENTAL CHAIR
"Make it happen!"
Dr. Bak Nguyen

0018
FROM THE POWER BEHIND THE ALPHA
"Humility is to know what you are and to recognize what you are not."
Dr. Bak Nguyen

0019
FROM MOMENTUM TRANSFER
"On thin ice, speed up, that's how you will eventually learn to fly!"
Dr. Bak Nguyen

0020
FROM MOMENTUM TRANSFER
"Control with wisdom is called influence."
Dr. Bak Nguyen

0021
FROM MOMENTUM TRANSFER
"To stabilize a momentum, speed up!"
Dr. Bak Nguyen

0022
FROM HYBRID
"Chords and patterns are the themes of the Universe."
Dr. Bak Nguyen

0023
FROM HYBRID
"A weakness is a strength out of reach."
Dr. Bak Nguyen

0024
FROM HYBRID
"Look for your next immediate win."
Dr. Bak Nguyen

0025
FROM REBOOT, TO GROW FROM MIDLIFE CRISIS
"Don't stop the flow of a river unless you are ready to clean up the flood."
Dr. Bak Nguyen

0026
FROM LEVERAGE COMMUNICATION INTO SUCCESS
"Find your worth in the service of others."
Dr. Bak Nguyen

0027
FROM LEVERAGE COMMUNICATION INTO SUCCESS
"Humility is not the denial of oneself but the acceptance of one true nature."
Dr. Bak Nguyen

0028
FROM THE BOOK OF LEGENDS, VOLUME 1
"We are all born little, as a chicken heart. If we keep an open mind, we will grow into a lion heart. Some will choose to be close-minded and will remain small."
Dr. Bak Nguyen

0029
FROM THE BOOK OF LEGENDS, VOLUME 1

"To have an open mind is step one.
To keep growing, one needs an open heart."

Dr. Bak Nguyen

0030
FROM THE BOOK OF LEGENDS, VOLUME 1

"Humility is the ability to recognize and to respect what we are, and stop pretending to be what we are not."

Dr. Bak Nguyen

0031
FROM SELFMADE

"Good things start to happen when you say yes!"

Dr. Bak Nguyen

0032
FROM SELFMADE

"Knowledge is the ground of the past.
Hope and Dreams are the air of the future."

Dr. Bak Nguyen

0033
FROM SELFMADE

"My deepest fear is to show up before God and not have enough to show for."

Dr. Bak Nguyen

0034
FROM THE RISE OF THE UNICORN
"To make the world a better place."
Dr. Bak Nguyen

0035
FROM THE RISE OF THE UNICORN
"A Momentum is when it is easier to keep moving than to stop."
Dr. Bak Nguyen

0036
FROM CHAMPION MINDSET
"I was open, and I bet on myself."
Dr. Bak Nguyen

0037
FROM HOW TO WRITE A BOOK IN 30 DAYS
"To keep Momentum, aim for the next win, as little as it might be."
Dr. Bak Nguyen

0038
FROM HOW TO WRITE A BOOK IN 30 DAYS
"A quote is a truth from another life, from a past legacy."
Dr. Bak Nguyen

0039
FROM HOW TO WRITE A BOOK IN 30 DAYS
"The fewer the words, the better."

Dr. Bak Nguyen

0040
FROM POWER, EMOTIONAL INTELLIGENCE
"Align your emotions and your ambitions to be whole, to be unstoppable."

Dr. Bak Nguyen

0041
FROM POWER, EMOTIONAL INTELLIGENCE
"I believe in myself, and I do it for God, not the other way around."

Dr. Bak Nguyen

0042
FROM BRANDING
"I kept the "Dr." on to remind me to always put your interests before mine."

Dr. Bak Nguyen

0043
FROM BRANDING
"Arrogance is not the bragging of our knowledge, but rather the denial of our ignorance."

Dr. Bak Nguyen

0044
FROM HORIZON VOLUME ONE
"I treat people, not teeth."

Dr. Bak Nguyen

0045
FROM THE POWER OF YES, VOLUME 1
"Writing books allowed me to evolve at the speed of my thoughts."

Dr. Bak Nguyen

0046
FROM THE POWER OF YES, VOLUME 1
"Speed is my power. Momentum, my expression."

Dr. Bak Nguyen

0047
FROM THE POWER OF YES VOLUME 3
"We do not need to choose, only to prioritize."

Dr. Bak Nguyen

0048
FROM HOW TO NOT FAIL AS A DENTIST
"Changing the world from a dental chair."

Dr. Bak Nguyen

0049
FROM HOW TO NOT FAIL AS A DENTIST
"I am not giving up, I am simply wising up!"

Dr. Bak Nguyen

0050
FROM HOW TO NOT FAIL AS A DENTIST
"With your money, do not trust anyone but yourself."

Dr. Bak Nguyen

0051
FROM HUMILITY FOR SUCCESS
"Reading will be cool again!"

Dr. Bak Nguyen

0052
FROM HUMILITY FOR SUCCESS
"Until it is done, it is air, good air but only air."

Dr. Bak Nguyen

0053
FROM MASTERMIND
"You can cheat, legally, by learning about shortcuts and leveraging."

Dr. Bak Nguyen

0054
FROM PLAYBOOK INTRODUCTION VOLUME 1
"Nothing will last forever, and nothing is free."
Dr. Bak Nguyen

0055
FROM PLAYBOOK INTRODUCTION VOLUME 2
"Be careful since doubts is a pet that you are feeding."
Dr. Bak Nguyen

0056
FROM PLAYBOOK INTRODUCTION VOLUME 2
"Reach for your next win as soon as possible, and build on it!"
Dr. Bak Nguyen

0057
FROM AMONGST THE ALPHAS, VOLUME 2
"Be bold, confident, and humble."
Dr. Bak Nguyen

0058
FROM AMONGST THE ALPHAS, VOLUME 2
"Growth happens at the giving end, not the receiving one."
Dr. Bak Nguyen

0059
FROM SUCCESS IS A CHOICE
"Be bold, be flexible, act fast and stay humble."
Dr. Bak Nguyen

0060
FROM SUCCESS IS A CHOICE
"To succeed, be flexible."
Dr. Bak Nguyen

0061
FROM 90 DAYS CHALLENGE
"In times of crisis, one has to reinvent oneself."
Dr. Bak Nguyen

0062
FROM RISING
"To matter, serve."
Dr. Bak Nguyen

0063
FROM RISING
"There is no free money."
Dr. Bak Nguyen

0064
FROM AFTERMATH
"For the first time of our lifetime, all the interests of the world are aligned."
Dr. Bak Nguyen

0065
FROM AFTERMATH
"In times of crisis, it is the perfect opportunity to reinvent who we are."
Dr. Bak Nguyen

0066
FROM AFTERMATH
"Yes, we can have it all!"
Dr. Bak Nguyen

0067
FROM TORNADO
"History will say that to celebrate one world record, we scored two more!"
Dr. Bak Nguyen

0068
FROM TORNADO
"The only way to keep overdelivering is playing, all-in!"
Dr. Bak Nguyen

0069
FROM TORNADO
"Dream and the means will come."
Dr. Bak Nguyen

0070
FROM ALPHA LADDERS VOLUME ONE
"All good things start with a YES."
Dr. Bak Nguyen

0071
FROM ALPHA LADDERS VOLUME 2
"Growth occurs at the giving end, always."
Dr. Bak Nguyen

0072
FROM THE CONFESSION OF AN OVERACHIEVER
"Being lazy doesn't mean that you don't have to do shit, it means that you don't have to go through shit to get things done."
Dr. Bak Nguyen

0073
FROM TO OVERACHIEVE EVERYTHING BEING LAZY
"Arrogance is not the recognition of who we are but the denial of what we are not."
Dr. Bak Nguyen

0074
FROM TO OVERACHIEVE EVERYTHING BEING LAZY
"You call me doctor to remind me to always put your needs before mine."
Dr. Bak Nguyen

0075
FROM TO OVERACHIEVE EVERYTHING BEING LAZY
"Nowadays, influence is power without liability."
Dr. Bak Nguyen

0076
FROM TO OVERACHIEVE EVERYTHING BEING LAZY
"I told you that everything in life is a trade. Be careful of what you are trading."
Dr. Bak Nguyen

0077
FROM SHORTCUT VOLUME 1 - HEALING
"Fear is a disease and it must be treated like one."
Dr. Bak Nguyen

This is **Shortcut volume 6, POWER**. Welcome to the Alphas.

Hammering air three times over and it will become steel.
Dr. BAK NGUYEN

CONCLUSION
by Dr. BAK NGUYEN

With this, we concluded the 6th volume of the **SHORTCUT series, POWER**. I warned you before we started that this is the darkest journey of the franchise. Dark because the temptations are real and very close.

The hurt and the pain will not be easily forgotten even if they can occur very quickly, not because we made a mistake or a false move, but simply because we doubted and hesitated.

> "Power is nature in force, vibrating through our body. Power is life and we are the vessels."
> Dr. Bak Nguyen

That's quote #2520. And power is dynamic, it is its nature. If we are serving it with all of our beings, we will become one with power. And that is when we will be empowered with superpowers, feeling that there is nothing we cannot do. We are in **synergy** with the universe, we are in the **zone**.

Being in synergy with the Universe is not a permanent state. As it has to be found, it can also be lost. The best way to keep the connection was to keep moving, serving more and more people so we can grow our hearts to contain more and more power.

If we lose focus, doubting or losing sight of WHY we a yielding such power, well, the power will burn the **bearer**. We are the bearer... and to heal from such burn is neither sure nor fast. Anyone burn from their own passion and power will tell you so.

Even worst, once power has left us, nothing is worst than the **feeling of void** we are left with as an empty vessel when once, not too long ago, we felt the power of the universe flowing in our veins. In common language, that is called **losing momentum**. What is left is the shadow of a man, the shadow of a woman who once were... a has been.

Is that a **greek tragedy** that cannot be avoided or a prophecy that can show us the way to take and the danger to avoid? Honestly, I don't know, and least not yet. I am still in power and much in momentum.

I know that I grew my momentum by an exponential factor for the last 4 years. I also know that if I stop here, the heat and power of the momentum will cause burns that I might never heal from. Fortunately, I have no intention to stop. On the contrary, I am speeding up, pacing up my pace, and impact.

I now jump faster and faster from one win to the next. Some win might take longer but I learnt very soon in my journey, never to discard or discount any win, as small as it might be. And to win, you need to walk that challenge first.

So that's my humility, no challenge is too small for me, just as no challenge is too big. I just need to assert if the next challenge is on my current trajectory or I will have to take a detour. Well, the detours are not always worth the time nor the pain. And that is how I chose my battles, on the detour, not the worth of that challenge.

Just like no challenge is too small, as I encounter a challenge bigger than I can swallow, once again, it is my humility that might save me from the fatal mistake of trying to swallow something too big for my mouth.

I am not backing down, I will just need to grow enough before coming back and tackle that exact challenge again. And I will come back since that is now a liability that I will have to carry around until I solve its mystery.

Yielding power, I learnt to stay as light as possible to keep moving forward. Yielding power, even if I am empowering others, serving them, well, soon enough jealousy will settle in. The only way I found not to face such resistance was moving through with speed, always faster and faster.

And to have speed, one needs confidence and to keep as light as possible. That's why we must learnt to leave our medals, victories, even talents behind to move forward only with what we need.

The longer you are hesitating to let go of your attachments, the harder it will be for you to keep up pace and momentum. Soon enough, your own powers will turn against you and burn you alive.

If you still needed to be convinced, well, know that you can not leave your liabilities behind, those are just stuck to your skin, until you have leveraged them into an opportunity and have solved their mysteries. Until then, you are stuck with your liabilities. Your only way to cut weight was to leave your medals and victories behind.

From there, as you are moving forward, you will find more and more powers to master and to yield. Each in their own time and timing. Enjoy that time yielding power, being one with that power.

Do what you came to do and then, gratefully and gracefully, clean up and polish your powers (talents) and leave them behind for the next one to come and find. If you wanted to gain momentum and speed, there is no better way. Keep moving and stay light.

You will grow much, yielding power after power. To keep moving, **Fun** is your key. To keep the fun in the game, you need to act as the dragons, to accept to unlearn and to be ready again, to start fresh. The dragons change shape with each power they master.

You too, will grow and gain the ability to change shape with each power you are merging with. If you wanted to fly, well, this is the way, growing from little to bigger, from a **chicken heart** into a **lion heart** and eventually, into a **dragon heart**.

Finding and yielding powers will be the journeys writing your legend. You will grow as you are serving more and more people, that's the how. Your legend is to do that much and to push that far. Well, that was your best way no to be burned.

Now that you know the pitfall and the darkness of power, you are ready to keep rising to your ultimate goal: happiness! And yes, Happiness is the 7th volume of the journey.

Until then, enjoy riding your powers and especially, do good! Greatness is not born nor given. It comes with doing more and better, jumping from win to win.

Surf your rise, reduce your liability and friction and leave your medal in the past. What will your power bring to our world next?

This is **Shortcut volume 6, POWER**. Welcome to the Alphas.

Hammering air three times over and it will become steel.

Dr. BAK NGUYEN

ANNEX
GLOSSARY OF Dr. BAK's LIBRARY

1

1SELF -080

REINVENT YOURSELF FROM ANY CRISIS
BY Dr. BAK NGUYEN

In 1SELF is about to reinvent yourself to rise from any crisis. Written in the midst of the COVID war, now more than ever, we need hope and the know-how to bridge the future. More than just the journey of Dr. Bak, this time, Dr. Bak is sharing his journey with mentors and people who built part of the world as we know it. Interviewed in this book, CHRISTIAN TRUDEAU, former CEO and FOUNDER of BCE EMERGIS (BELL CANADA), he also digitalized the Montreal Stock Exchange. RON KLEIN, American Innovator, inventor of the magnetic stripe of the credit card, of MLS (Multi-listing services) and the man who digitalized WALL STREET bonds markets. ANDRE CHATELAIN, former first vice-president of the MOVEMENT DES JARDINS. Dr. JEAN DE SERRES, former CEO of HEMA QUEBEC. These men created billions in values and have changed our lives, even without us knowing. They all come together to share their experiences and knowledge to empower each and everyone to emerge stronger from this crisis, from any crisis.

AFTERMATH -063
BUSINESS AFTER THE GREAT PAUSE
BY Dr. BAK NGUYEN & Dr. ERIC LACOSTE

In AFTERMATH, Dr. Bak joins forces with Community leader and philanthrope Dr. Eric Lacoste. Two powerful minds and forces of nature in the reaction to the worst economic meltdown in modern times. We are all victims of the CORONA virus. Both just like humans have learned to adapt to survive, so is our economy. Most business structures and management philosophies are inherited from the age of industrialization and beyond. COVID-19 has shot down the world economy with months. At the time of the AFTERMATH, the truth is many corporations and organizations will either have to upgrade to the INFORMATION AGE or disappear. More than the INFORMATION upgrade, the era of SOCIAL MEDIA and the MILLENNIALS are driving a revolution in the core philosophy of all organizations. Profit is not king anymore, support is. In this time and age where a teenager with a social account can compete with the million dollars PR firm, social implication is now the new cornerstone. Those who will adapt will prevail and prosper, while the resistance and old guards will soon be forgotten as fossils of a past era.

ALPHA LADDERS -075
CAPTAIN OF YOUR DESTINY
BY Dr. BAK NGUYEN & JONAS DIOP

In ALPHA LADDERS, Dr. Bak is sharing his private conversation and board meetings with 2 of his trusted lieutenants, strategist Jonas Diop and international Counsellor, Brenda Garcia. As both the Dr. Bak and ALPHA brands are gaining in popularity and traction, it was time to get the movement to the next level. Now, it's about building a community and to help everyone willing to become ALPHAS to find their powers. Dr. Bak is a natural recruiter of ALPHAS and peers. He also spent the last 20 years plus, training and mentoring proteges. Now comes the time to empower more and more proteges to become ALPHAS. ALPHAS LADDERS is the journey of how Dr. Bak went from a product of Conformity to rise into a force of Nature, know as a kind tornado. In ALPHA LADDERS Jonas pushed Dr. Bak to retrace each of the steps of his awakening, steps that we can breakdown and reproduce for ourselves. The goal is to empower each willing individual to become the ultimate Captain of his or her destiny, and to do it, again and again. Welcome to the Alphas.

ALPHA LADDERS 2 -081
SHAPING LEADERS AND ACHIEVERS
BY Dr. BAK NGUYEN & BRENDA GARCIA

In ALPHA LADDERS 2, Dr. Bak is sharing the second part of his private conversation and board meetings with his trusted lieutenants. This time it is with international Counsellor, Brenda Garcia that the dialogue is taking place. In this second tome, the journey is taken to the next level. If the first tome was about the WHYs and the HOWs at an individual level, this tome is about the WHYs and the HOWs at the societal level. Through the lens of her background in international relations and diplomacy, Brenda now has the mission to help Dr. Bak establish structures, not only for his emerging organization and legacy, THE ALPHAS, but to also inspire all the other leaders and structures of our society. To do this, Brenda is taking Dr. Bak on an anthropological, sociological and philosophical journey to revisit different historical key moments in various fields and eras, going as far back as in ancient Greece at the dawn of democracy, all the way to the golden era of modern multilateralism embodied by the UN structure. Learning from the legacies of prominent figures going from Plato to Ban Ki Moon, Martin Luther King or Nelson Mandela, to Machiavelli, Marx and Simone de Beauvoir, Brenda and Dr. Bak are attempting to grasp the essence of structure and hierarchy, their goal being to empower each willing individual to become the ultimate Captain of their own success, to climb up the ladders no matter how high it is, and to build their legacy one step at a time.

AMONGST THE ALPHAS -058
BY Dr. BAK NGUYEN, with Dr. MARIA KUNDSTATER, Dr. PAUL OUELLETTE and Dr. JEREMY KRELL

In AMONGST THE ALPHAS Dr. Bak opens the blueprint of the next level with the hope that everyone can be better, bigger, wiser, but above all, a philosophy of Life that if, well applied, can bring inspiration to life. The Alphas rose in the midst of the COVID war as an International Collaboration to empower individuals to rise from the global crisis. Joining Dr. Bak are some of the world thinkers and achievers, the Alphas. Doctors, business people, thinkers, achievers, influencers, they are coming together to define what is an Alpha and his or her role, making the world a better place. This isn't the American dream, it is the human dream, one that can help you make History.Joining Dr. Bak are 3 Alpha authors, Dr. Maria Kundstater, Dr. Paul Ouellette and Dr. Jeremy Krell. This book started with questions from coach Jonas Diop. Welcome to the Alphas.

AMONGST THE ALPHAS vol.2 -059
ON THE OTHER SIDE
BY Dr. BAK NGUYEN with Dr. JULIO REYNAFARJE, Dr. LINA DUSEVICIUTE and Dr. DUC-MINH LAM-DO

In AMONGST THE ALPHAS 2, Dr. Bak continues to explore the meaning of what it is to be an Alpha and how to act amongst Alphas, because as the saying taught us: alone one goes fast, together we goes far. Some people see the problem. Some people look at the problem, some people created the problem. Some people leverage the problem into solutions and opportunities. Well, all of those people are Alphas. Networking and leveraging one another, their powers and reach are beyond measure. And one will keep the other in line too. Joining Dr. Bak are 3 Alphas from around the world coming together to share and collaborate, Dr. DUSEVICIUTE, Dr. LAM-DO and Dr. REYNAFARJE. This isn't the American dream, it is the human dream, one that can help you make History. Welcome to the Alphas.

B

BOOTCAMP -071
BOOKS TO REWRITE MINDSETS INTO WINNING STATES OF MIND
BY Dr. BAK NGUYEN

In BOOTCAMP 8 BOOKS TO REWRITE MINDSETS INTO WINNING STATES OF MIND, Dr. Bak is taking you into his past, before the visionary entrepreneur, before the world records, before the Industry's disruptor status. Here are 8 of the books that changed Dr. Bak's thinking and, therefore, reset his evolution into the course we now know him for. BOOTCAMP: 8 BOOKS TO REWRITE MINDSETS INTO WINNING STATES OF MIND, is a Bootcamp of 8 weeks for anyone looking to experience Dr. Bak's training to become THE Dr. BAK you came to know and love. This book will summarize how each title changed Dr. Bak mindset into a state of mind and how he applied that to rewrite his destiny. 8 books to read, that's 8 weeks of Bootcamp to access the power of your MIND and of your WILL. Are you ready for a change?

BRANDING -044
BALANCING STRATEGY AND EMOTIONS
BY Dr. BAK NGUYEN

BRANDING is communication to its most powerful state. Branding is not just about communicating anymore but about making a promise, about establishing a relation, about generating an emotion. More than once, Dr. Bak proved himself to be a master, communicating and branding his ideas into flags attracting interest and influences, nationally and internationally. In BRANDING, Dr. Bak shares a very unique and personal journey, branding Dr. Bak. How does he go from Dr. Nguyen, a loved and respected dentist to becoming Dr. Bak, a world anchor hosting THE ALPHAS in the medical and financial world? More than a personal journey, BRANDING helps to break down the steps to elevate someone with nothing else but the force of his or her spirit. Welcome to the Alphas.

CHANGING THE WORLD FROM A DENTAL CHAIR -007
BY Dr. BAK NGUYEN

Since he has received the EY's nomination for entrepreneur of the year for his startup Mdex & Co, Dr. Bak Nguyen has pushed the opportunity to the next level. Speaker, author, and businessman, Dr. Bak is a true entrepreneur and industries' disruptor. To compensate for the startup's status of Mdex & Co, he challenged himself to write a book based on the EY's questionnaire to share an in-depth vision of his company. With "Changing the World from a dental chair". Dr. Bak is sharing his thought process and philosophy to his approach to the industry. Not looking to revolutionize but rather to empower, he became, despite himself, an industries disruptor: an entrepreneur who has established a new benchmark. Dr. Bak Nguyen is a cosmetic dentist and visionary businessman who won the GRAND HOMAGE prize of "LYS de la Diversité" 2016, for his contribution as a citizen and entrepreneur in the community. He also holds recognitions from the Canadian Parliament and the Canadian Senate.

In 2003, he founded Mdex, a dental company upon which in 2018, he launched the most ambitious private endeavour to reform the dental industry, Canada wide. He wrote seven books covering ENTREPRENEURSHIP, LEADERSHIP, QUEST of IDENTITY, and now, PROFESSION HEALTH. Philosopher, he has close to his heart the quest happiness of the people surrounding him, patients, and colleagues alike. Those projects have allowed Dr. Nguyen to attract interests from the international and diplomatic community and he is now the centre of a global discussion on the wellbeing and the future of the health profession. It is in that matter that he shares with you his thoughts and encourages the health community to share their own stories.

CHAMPION MINDSET -039
LEARNING TO WIN
BY Dr. BAK NGUYEN & CHRISTOPHE MULUMBA

CHAMPION MINDSET is the encounter of the business world and the professional sports world. Industries' Disruptor Dr. BAK NGUYEN shares his wisdom and views with the HAMMER, CFL Football Star, Edmonton's Eskimos CHRISTOPHE MULUMBA on how to leverage on the champion mindset to create successful entrepreneurs. Writing and challenging each other, they discovered the parallels and the difference of both worlds, but mainly, the recipe for leveraging from one to succeed in the other, from champions and entrepreneurs to WINNERS. Build and score your millions, it is a matter of mindset! This is CHAMPION MINDSET.

EMPOWERMENT -069
BY Dr. BAK NGUYEN

In EMPOWERMENT, Dr. Bak's 69th book, writing a book every 8 days for 8 weeks in a row to write the next world record of writing 72 books/36 months, Dr. Bak is taking a rest, sharing his inner feelings, inspiration, and motivation. Much more than his dairy, EMPOWERMENT is the key to walk in his footsteps and to comprehend the process of an overachiever. Dr. Bak's helped and inspired countless people to find their voice, to live their dream, and to be the better version of themselves. Why is he sharing as much and keep sharing? Why is he going that fast, always further and further, why and how is he keeping his inspiration and momentum? Those are all the answers EMPOWERMENT will deliver to you. This book might be one of the fastest Dr. Bak has written, not because of time constraints but from inspiration, pure inspiration to share and to grow. There is always a dark side to each power, two faces to a coin. Well, this is the less prominent facets of Dr. Bak Momentum and success, the road to his MINDSET.

FORCES OF NATURE -015
FORGING THE CHARACTER OF WINNERS
BY Dr. BAK NGUYEN

In FORCES OF NATURE, Dr. Bak is giving his all. This is his 15 books written within 15 months. It is the end of a marathon to set the next world record. For the occasion, he wanted to end with a big bang! How about a book with all of his biggest challenges? A Quest of Identity, a journey looking for his name and powers, Dr. Bak is borrowing with myths and legends to make this journey universal. Yes, this is Dr. Bak's mythology. Demons, heroes and Gods, there are forces of Nature that we all meet on our way for our name. Some will scare us, some will fight us, some will manipulate us. We can flee, we can hide, we can fight. What we do will define our next encounter and the one after. A tale of personal growth, a journey to find power and purpose, Dr. Bak is showing us the path to freedom, the Path of Life. Welcome to the Alphas.

HORIZON, BUILDING UP THE VISION -045
VOLUME ONE
BY Dr. BAK NGUYEN

Dr. Bak is opening up at your demand! Many of you are following Dr. Bak online and are asking to know more about his lifestyle. This is how he has chosen to respond: sharing his lifestyle as he traveled the world and what he learned in each city to come to build his Mindset as a driver and a winner. Here are 10 destinations (over 69 that will be following in the next volumes...) in which he shares his journey. New York, Quebec, Paris, Punta Cana, Monaco, Los Angeles, Nice, Holguin, the journey happened over twenty years.

HORIZON, ON THE FOOTSTEP OF TITANS -048
VOLUME TWO
BY Dr. BAK NGUYEN

Dr. Bak is opening up at your demand! Many of you are following Dr. Bak online and are asking to know more about his lifestyle. This is how he has chosen to respond: sharing his lifestyle as he traveled the world and what he learned in each city to come to build his Mindset as a driver and a winner. Here are 9 destinations (over 72 that will be following in the next volumes...) in which he shares his journey. Hong Kong, London, Rome, San Francisco, Anaheim, and more..., the journey happened over twenty years. Dr. Bak is sharing with you his feelings, impressions, and how they shaped his state of mind and character into Dr. Bak. From a dreamer to a driver and a builder, the journey started since he was 3. Wealth is a state of mind, and a state of mind is the basis of the drive. Find out about the mind of an Industry's disruptor.

HORIZON, Dr.EAMING OF THE FUTURE -068
VOLUME THREE
BY Dr. BAK NGUYEN

Dr. Bak is back. From the midst of confinement, he remembers and writes about what life was, when traveling was a natural part of Life. It will come back. Now more than ever, we need to open both our hearts and minds to fight fear and intolerance. Writing from a time of crisis, he is sharing the magic and psychological effect of seeing the world and how it has shaped his mindset. Here are 9 other destinations (over 75) in which he shares his journey. Beijing, Key West, Madrid, Amsterdam, Marrakech and more..., the journey happened over twenty years.

HOW TO NOT FAIL AS A DENTIST -047
BY Dr. BAK NGUYEN

In HOW TO NOT FAIL AS A DENTIST, Dr. Bak is given 20 plus years of experience and knowledge of what it is to be a dentist on the ground. PROFESSIONAL INTELLIGENCE, FINANCIAL INTELLIGENCE and MANAGEMENT INTELLIGENCE are the fields that any dentist will have to master for a chance to success and a shot for happiness practicing dentistry. Where ever you are starting your career as a new graduate or a veteran in the field looking to reach the next level, this is book smart and street smart all into one. This is Million Dollar Mindset applied to dentistry. We won't be making a millionaire out of you from this book, we will be giving you a shot to happiness and success. The million will follow soon enough.

HOW TO WRITE A BOOK IN 30 DAYS -042
BY Dr. BAK NGUYEN

In HOW TO WRITE YOUR BOOK IN 30 DAYS, Dr. Bak has crafted writing skills and techniques that can be shared and mastered. This book is mainly about structure and how to keep moving forward, avoiding the hit of the INSPIRATION WALL. You will find a wealth of wisdom from his experience writing your first, second, or even 10th book. Dr. Bak is sharing his secrets writing books, having written himself 72 books within 36 months. Visionary businessman, doctor in dentistry, Dr. Bak describes himself as a Dentist by circumstances, a communicator by passion, and an entrepreneur by nature.

HOW TO WRITE A SUCCESSFUL BUSINESS PLAN -049
BY Dr. BAK NGUYEN & ROUBA SAKR

In HOW TO WRITE A SUCCESSFUL BUSINESS PLAN, Dr. Bak is given 20 plus years of experience and knowledge of what it is to be an entrepreneur and more importantly, how to have the investors and banks on your side. Being an entrepreneur is surely not something you learn from school, but there are steps to master so you can communicate your views and vision. That's the only way you will have financing. Writing a business is only not a mandatory stop only for the bankers, but an essential step to every entrepreneur, to know the direction and what's coming next. A business plan is also not set in stone, if there is a truth in business is that nothing will go as planned. Writing down your business plan the first time will prepare you to adapt and to overcome the challenges and surprises. For most entrepreneurs, a business is a passion. To most investors and all banks, a business is a system. Your business plan is the map to that system. However unique your ideas and business are, the mapping follows the same steps and pattern.

HUMILITY FOR SUCCESS -051
BALANCING STRATEGY AND EMOTIONS
BY Dr. BAK NGUYEN

HUMILITY FOR SUCCESS is exploring the emotional discomforts and challenges champions, and overachievers put themselves through. Success is never done overnight and on the way, just like the pain and the struggles aren't enough, we are dealing with the doubts, the haters, and those who like to tell us how to live our lives and what to do. At the same time, nothing of worth can be achieved alone. Every legend has a cast of characters, allies, mentors, companions, rivals, and foes. So one needs the key to social behaviour. HUMILITY FOR SUCCESS is exploring the matter and will help you sort out beliefs from values, peers from friends. Humility is much more about how we see ourselves than how others see us. For any entrepreneur and champion, our daily is to set our mindset right, and to perfect our skills, not to fit in. There is a world where CONFIDENCE grows is in synergy with HUMILITY. As you set the right label on the right belief, you will be able to grow and to leave the lies and haters far behinds. This is HUMILITY FOR SUCCESS.

HYBRID -011
THE MODERN QUEST OF IDENTITY
BY Dr. BAK NGUYEN

IDENTITY -004
THE ANTHOLOGY OF QUESTS
BY Dr. BAK NGUYEN

What if John Lennon was still alive and running for president today? What kind of campaign will he be running? IDENTIFY -THE ANTHOLOGY OF QUESTS is about the quest each of us has to undertake, sooner or later, THE QUEST OF IDENTITY. Citizen of the world, aim to be one, the one, one whole, one unity, made of many. That's the anthology of life! Start with your one, find your unity, and your legend will start. We are all small-minded people anyway! We need each other to be one! We need each other to be happy, so we, so you, so I, can be happy. This is the chorus of life. This is our song! Citizens of the world, I salute you! This is the first tome of the IDENTITY QUEST. FORCES OF NATURE (tome 2) will be following in SUMMER 2021. Also under development, Tome 3 - THE CONQUEROR WITHIN will start production soon.

INDUSTRIES DISRUPTORS -006
BY Dr. BAK NGUYEN

INDUSTRIES DISRUPTORS is a strange title, one that sparkles mixed feelings. A disruptor is someone making a difference, and since we, in general, do not like change, the label is mostly negative. But a disruptor is mostly someone who sees the same problem and challenge from another angle. The disruptor will tackle that angle and come up with something new from something existent. That's evolution! In INDUSTRIES DISRUPTORS, Dr. Bak is joining forces with James Stephan-Usypchuk to share with us what is going on in the minds and shoes of those entrepreneurs disrupting the old habits. Dr. Bak is changing the world from a dental chair, disrupting the dental, and now the book industry. James is a maverick in the Intelligence space, from marketing to Artificial Intelligence. Coming from very different backgrounds and industries, they end up telling very similar stories. If disruptors change the world, well, their story proves that disruptors can be made and forged. Here's the recipe. Here are their stories.

K

KRYPTO -040
TO SAVE THE WORLD
BY Dr. BAK NGUYEN & ILYAS BAKOUCH

L

LEADERSHIP -003
PANDORA'S BOX
BY Dr. BAK NGUYEN

LEADERSHIP, PANDORA'S BOX is 21 presidential speeches for a better tomorrow for all of us. It aims to drive HOPE and motivation into each and every one of us. Together we can make the difference, we hold such power. Covering themes from LOYALTY to GENEROSITY, from FREEDOM and INTELLIGENCE to DOUBTS and DEATH, this is not the typical presidential or motivational speeches that we are used to. LEADERSHIP PANDORA'S BOX will surf your emotions first, only to dive with you to touch the core and soul of our meaning: to matter. This is not a Quest of Identity, but the cry to rally as a species, to raise our heads toward the future, and to move forward as a WHOLE. Not a typical Dr. Bak's book, LEADERSHIP, PANDORA'S BOX is a must-read for all of you looking for hope and purpose, all of us, citizens of the world.

LEVERAGE -014
COMMUNICATION INTO SUCCESS
BY Dr. BAK NGUYEN

In LEVERAGE COMMUNICATION TO SUCCESS, Dr. Bak shares his secret and mindsets to elevate an idea into a vision and a vision into an endeavour. Some endeavours will be a project, some others will become companies, and some will grow into a movement. It does not matter, each started with great communication.Communication is a very vast concept, education, sale, sharing, empowering, coaching, preaching, entertaining. Those are all different kinds of communication. The intent differs, the audiences vary, the messages are unique but the frame can be templated and mastered. In LEVERAGE COMMUNICATION TO SUCCESS, Dr. Bak is loyal to his core, sharing only what he knows best, what he has done himself. This book is dedicated to communicating successfully in business.

MASTERMIND, 7 WAYS INTO THE BIG LEAGUE -052
BY Dr. BAK NGUYEN & JONAS DIOP

MASTERMIND, 7 WAYS INTO THE BIG LEAGUE is the result of the encounter of business coach Jonas Diop and Dr. Bak. As a professional podcaster and someone always seeking the truth and ways to leverage success and performance, coach Jonas is putting Dr. Bak to the test, one that should reveal his secret to overachieve month after month, accumulating a new world record every month. Follow those two great minds as they push each other to surpass themselves, each in their own way and own style. MASTERMIND, 7 WAYS INTO THE BIG LEAGUE is more than a roadmap to success, it is a journey and a live testimony as you are turning the pages, one by one.

MIDAS TOUCH -065
POST-COVID DENTISTRY
BY Dr. BAK NGUYEN, Dr. JULIO REYNAFARJE AND Dr. PAUL OUELLETTE

MIDAS TOUCH, is the memoir of what happened in the ALPHAS SUMMIT in the midst of the GREAT PAUSE as great minds throughout the world in the dental field are coming together. As the time of competition is obsolete, the new era of collaboration is blooming. This is the 3rd book of the ALPHAS, after AFTERMATH and RELEVANCY, all written in the midst of confinement. Dr. Julio Reynafarje is bearing this initiative, to share with you the secret of a successful and lasting relationship with your patients, balancing science and psychology, kindness, and professionalism. He personally invited the ALPHAS to join as co-author, Dr. Paul Ouellette, and Dr.

Paul Dominique, and Dr. Bak.Together, they have more than 100 years of combined experience, wisdom, trade, skills, philosophy, and secrets to share with you to empower you in the rebuilding of the dental profession in the aftermath of COVID. RELEVANCY was about coming together and to rebuild the future. MIDAS TOUCH is about how to build, one treatment plan at a time, one story at a time, one smile at a time.

MINDSET ARMORY -050
BY Dr. BAK NGUYEN

MINDSET ARMORY is Dr. Bak's 49th book, days after he completed his world record of writing 48 books within 24 months, on top of being a CEO of Mdex & Co and a full-time cosmetic dentist. Dr. Bak is undoubtedly an OVERACHIEVER. From his last books, he has shared more and more of his lifestyle and how it forged his winning mindset. Within MINDSET ARMORY, Dr. Bak is sharing with us his tools, how he found them, forged them, and leverage them. Just like any warrior needs a shield, a sword, and a ride, here are Dr. Bak's. For any entrepreneur, the road to success is a long and winding journey. On the way, some will find allies and foes. Some allies will become foes, and some foes might become allies. In today's competitive world, the only constant is change. With the right tool, it is possible to achieve. The right tool, the right mindset. This is MINDSET ARMORY.

MIRROR -085
BY Dr. BAK NGUYEN

MIRROR is the theme for a personal book. Not only to Dr. Bak but to all of us looking to reach beyond who and what we actually are. MIRROR is special in the fact that it is not only the content of the book that is of worth but the process in which Dr. Bak shared his own evolution. To go beyond who we are, one must grow every day. And how do you compare your growth and how far have you reach? Looking in the mirror. In all of Dr. Bak's writing, looking at the past is a trap to avoid at all costs. Looking in the mirror, is that any better? Share Dr. Bak's way to push and keep pushing himself without friction nor resistance. Please read that again. To evolve without friction or resistance... that is the source of infinite growth and the unification of the Quest for Power and the Quest of Happiness.

MOMENTUM TRANSFER -009
BY Dr. BAK NGUYEN & Coach DINO MASSON

How to be successful in your business and in your life? Achieve Your Biggest Goals With MOMENTUM TRANSFER. START THE BUSINESS YOU WANT - AND BRING IT NEXT LEVEL! GET THE LIFE YOU ALWAYS WANTED - AND IMPROVE IT! TAKE ANY PROJECTS YOU HAVE - AND MAKE IT THE BEST! In this powerful book, you'll discover what a small business owner learned from a millionaire and successful entrepreneur. He applied his mentor's principles and is explaining them in full detail in this book. The small business owner wrote the book he has always wanted to read and went from the verge of bankruptcy to quadrupling his revenues in less than 9 months and improve his personal life by increasing his energy and bring back peacefulness. Together, the millionaire and the small business owner are sharing their most valuable business and life lessons to the world. The most powerful book to increase your momentum in your business and your life introduces simple and radical life-changing concepts: Multiply your business revenues by finding the Eye of your Momentum - Increase your energy by building and feeding your own Momentum - How to increase your confidence with these simple steps - How to transfer your new powerful energy into other aspects of your business and life - How to set goals and achieve them (even crush them!)- How to always tap into an effortless and limitless force within you- And much, much more!

PLAYBOOK INTRODUCTION -055
BY Dr. BAK NGUYEN

In PLAYBOOK INTRODUCTION, Dr. Bak is open the door to all the newcomers and aspirant entrepreneurs who are looking at where and when to start. Based on questions of two college students wanting to know how to start their entrepreneurial journey, Dr. Bak dives into his experiences to empower the next generation, not about what they should do, but how he, Dr. Bak, would have done it today. This is an important aspect to recognize in the business world, the world has changed since the INFORMATION AGE and the advent of the millenniums into the market. Most matrix and know-how have to be adapted to today's speed and accessibility to the information. We are living at the INFORMATION AGE, this book is the precursor to the ABUNDANCE AGE, at least to those open to embrace the opportunity.

PLAYBOOK INTRODUCTION 2 -056
BY Dr. BAK NGUYEN

In PLAYBOOK INTRODUCTION 2, Dr. Bak continuing the journey to welcome the newcomers and aspirant entrepreneurs looking at where and when to start. If the first volume covers the mindset, the second is covering much more in-depth the concept of debt and leverage. This is an important aspect to recognize in the business world, the world has changed since the INFORMATION AGE and the advent of the millenniums into the market. Most matrix and know-how have to be adapted to today's speed and accessibility to the information. We are living at the INFORMATION AGE, this book is the precursor to the ABUNDANCE AGE, at least to those open to embrace the opportunity.

POWER -043
EMOTIONAL INTELLIGENCE
BY Dr. BAK NGUYEN

IN POWER, EMOTIONAL INTELLIGENCE, Dr. Bak is sharing his experiences and secrets leveraging on his EMOTIONAL INTELLIGENCE, a power we all have within. From SYMPATHY, having others opening up to you, to ACTIVE LISTENING, saving you time and energy; from EMPATHY, allowing you to predict the future to INFLUENCE, enabling you to draft the future, not to forget the power of the crowd with MOMENTUM, you are now in possession of power in tune with nature, yourself. It is a unique take on the subject to empower you to find your powers and your destiny. Visionary businessman, doctor in dentistry, Dr. Bak describes himself as a Dentist by circumstances, a communicator by passion, and an entrepreneur by nature.

POWERPLAY -078
HOW TO BUILD THE PERFECT TEAM
BY Dr. BAK NGUYEN

In POWERPLAY, HOW TO BUILD THE PERFECT TEAM, Dr. Bak is sharing with you his experience, perspective, and mistake traveling the journey of the entrepreneur. A serial entrepreneur himself, he started venture only with a single partner as team to build companies with a director of human resources and a board of directors. POWERPLAY is not a story, it is the HOW TO build the perfect team, knowing that perfection is a lie. So how can one build a team that will empower his or her vision? How to recruit, how to train, how to retain? Those are all legitimate questions. And all of those won't matter if the first question isn't answered: what is the reason for the team? There is the old way to hire and the new way to recruit. Yes, Human Resources is all about mindset too! This journey is one of introspection, of leadership, and a cheat sheet to build, not only the perfect team but the team that will empower your legacy to the next level.

PROFESSION HEALTH - TOME ONE -005
THE UNCONVENTIONAL QUEST OF HAPPINESS
BY Dr. BAK NGUYEN, Dr. MIRJANA SINDOLIC, Dr. ROBERT DURAND AND COLLABORATORS

Why are health professionals burning out while they give the best of themselves to heal the world? Dr. Bak aims to break the curse of isolation that health professionals face and establish a conversation to start the healing process. PROFESSION HEALTH is the basis of an ongoing discussion and will also serve as an introduction to a study lead by Professor Robert Durand, DMD, MSc Science from University of Montreal, study co-financed by Mdex and the Federal Government of Canada. Co-writers are Dr. Mirjana Sindolic, Professor Robert Durand, Dr. Jean De Serres, MD and former President of Hema Quebec, Counsel-Minister Luis Maria Kalaff Sanchez, Dr. Miguel Angel Russo, MD, Banker Anthony Siggia, Banker Kyles Yves, and more...
This is the first Tome of three, dedicated to help "WHITE COATS" to heal and to find their happiness.

R

REBOOT -012
MIDLIFE CRISIS
BY Dr. BAK NGUYEN

MidLife Crisis is a common theme to each of us as we reach the threshold. As a man, as a woman, why is it that half of the marriages end up in recall? If anything else would have half those rates of failure, the lawsuits would be raining. Where are the flaws, the traps? Love is strong and pure, why is marriage not the reflection of that? All hard to ask questions with little or no answers. Dr. Bak is sharing his reflections and findings as he reached himself the WALL OF MARRIAGE. This is a matter that affects all of our lives. It is time for some answers.

RELEVANCY - TOME TWO -064
REINVENTING OURSELVES TO SURVIVE
BY Dr. BAK NGUYEN & Dr. PAUL OUELLETTE AND COLLABORATORS

THE GREAT PAUSE was a reboot of all the systems of society. Many outdated systems will not make it back. The Dental Industry is a needed one, it has laid on complacency for far too long. In an age where expertise is global and democratized and can be replaced with technologies and artificial intelligence, the REBOOT will force, not just an update, but an operating system replacement and a firmware upgrade. First, they saved their industry with THE ALPHAS INITIATIVE, sharing their knowledge and vision freely to all the world's dental industry. With the OUELLETTE INITIATIVE, they bought some time to all the dental clinics to resume and to adjust. The warning has been given, the clock is now ticking. who will prevail and prosper and who will be left behind, outdated and obsolete?

RISING -062
TO WIN MORE THAN YOU ARE AFRAID TO LOSE
BY Dr. BAK NGUYEN

In RISING, TO WIN MORE TAN YOU ARE AFRAID TO LOSE, Dr. Bak is breaking down the strategy to success to all, not only those wearing white coats and scrubs. More than his previous book (SUCCESS IS A CHOICE), this one is covering most of the aspects of getting to the next level, psychologically, socially, and financially. Rising is broken down into three key strategies: Financial Leverage - Compressing time - Always being in control. Presented by MILLION DOLLAR MINDSET, the book is covering more than the ways to create wealth, but also how to reach happiness and to live a life without regrets. Dr. Bak the CEO and founder of Mdex & Co, a company with the promise of reforming the whole dental industry for the better. He wrote more than 60 books within 30 months as he is sharing his experiences, secrets, and wisdom.

S

SELFMADE -036
GRATITUDE AND HUMILITY
BY Dr. BAK NGUYEN

This is the story of Dr. Bak, an artist who became a dentist, a dentist who became an Entrepreneur, an Entrepreneur who is seeking to save an entire industry. In his free time, Dr. Bak managed to write 37 books and is a contender to 3 world records to be confirmed. Businessman and visionary, his views and philosophy are ahead of our time. This is his 37th book. In SELFMADE, Dr. Bak is answering the questions most entrepreneurs want to know, the HOWTO and the secret recipes, not just to succeed, but to keep going no matter what! SELFMADE is the perfect read for any entrepreneurs, novices, and veterans.

SHORTCUT vol. 1 - HEALING -093
BY Dr. BAK NGUYEN

In SHORTCUT 408 HEALING QUOTES, Dr. Bak revisits and compiles his journey of healing and growing. Just anyone, he was molded and shaped by Conformity and Society to the point of blending and melting. Walking his journey of healing, he rediscovers himself and found his true calling. And once whole with himself and with the Universe, Dr. Bak found his powers. In SHORTCUT 408 HEALING QUOTES, you have a quick and easy way to surf his mindsets and what allowed him to heal, to find back his voice and wings, and to walk his destiny. You too are walking your Quest of Identity. That one is mainly a journey of healing. May you find yours and your powers.

SHORTCUT vol. 2 - GROWING -094
BY Dr. BAK NGUYEN

In SHORTCUT 408 GROWTH QUOTES, Dr. Bak is compiling his library of books about personal growth and self-improvement. More than a motivational book, more than a compilation of knowledge, Dr. Bak is sharing the mindsets upon which he found his power to achieve and to overachieve. We all have our powers, only they were muted and forgotten as we were forged by Conformity and Society. After the healing process, walking your Quest of Identity, the Quest for you growth and God given power is next to lead you to walk your Destiny.

SHORTCUT vol. 3 - LEADERSHIP -095
BY Dr. BAK NGUYEN

In SHORTCUT 365 LEADERSHIP QUOTES, Dr. Bak is compiling his library of books about leadership and ambition. Yes, the ambition is to find your worth and to make the world a better place for all of us. If the 3rd volume of SHORTCUT is mainly a motivational compilation, it also holds the secrets and mindsets to influence and leadership. If you were looking to walk your legend and to impact the world, you are walking a lonely path.

You might on your own, but it does not have to be harder than it is. As we all have your unique challenges, the key to victory is often found in the same place, your heart. And here are 365 shortcuts to keep you believing and to attract more people to you as you are growing into a true leader.

SHORTCUT vol. 4 - CONFIDENCE -096
BY Dr. BAK NGUYEN

SHORTCUT 518 CONFIDENCE QUOTES, is the most voluminous compilation of Dr. Bak's quotes. To heal was the first step. To grow and find your powers came next. As you are walking your personal legend, Confidence is both your sword and armour to conquer your Destiny and to overcome all of the challenges on your way. In SHORTCUT volume four, Dr. Bak comprises all his mindsets and wisdom to ease your ascension. Confidence is not something one is simply born with, but something to nurture, grow, and master. Some will have the chance to be raised by people empowering Confidence, others will have to heal from Conformity to grow their confidence. It does not matter, only once Confident, can one stand tall and see clearly the horizon.

SHORTCUT vol. 5- SUCCESS -097
BY Dr. BAK NGUYEN

Success is not a destination but a journey and a side effect. While no map can lead you to success, the right mindset will forge your own success, the one without medals nor labels. If you are looking to walk your legend, to be successful is merely the beginning. Actually, being successful is often a side effect of the mindsets and actions that you took, you provoked. In SHORTCUT 317 SUCCESS QUOTES, Dr. Bak is revisiting his journey, breaking down what led him to be successful despite the odds stacked against him. As success is the consequence of mindsets, choices, and actions, it can be duplicated over and over again, one just needs to master the mindsets first.

SHORTCUT vol. 6- POWER -098
BY Dr. BAK NGUYEN

That's the kind of power that you will discover within this journey. Power is a tool, a leverage. Well used, it will lead to great achievements. Misused, it will be your downfall. If a sword sometimes has 2 edges, Power is a sword with no handle and multiple edges. You have been warned. In SHORTCUT 376 POWER QUOTES, Dr. Bak is compiling all the powers he found and mastered walking his own legend. If the first power was Confidence, very quickly, Dr. Bak realized that Confidence was the key to many, many more powers. Where to find them, how to yield them, and how to leverage these powers is the essence of the 6th volume of SHORTCUT.

SHORTCUT vol. 7- HAPPINESS -099
BY Dr. BAK NGUYEN

We were all born happy and then, somehow, we lost our ways and forgot our ways home. Is this the real tragedy behind the lost paradise myth? If we were happy once, we can trust our heart to find our way home, once more. This is the journey of the 7th volume of the SHORTCUT series. In SHORTCUT 306 HAPPINESS QUOTES, Dr. Bak is revisiting and compiling all the secrets and mindsets leading to happiness. Happiness is not just a destination but a shrine for Confidence and a safe place to regroup, to heal, to grow. We each have our own happiness. What you will learn here is where to find yours and, more importantly, how to leverage you to ease the journey ahead, because happiness is not your final destination. It can be the key to your legend.

SHORTCUT vol. 8- DOCTORS -100
BY Dr. BAK NGUYEN

If healing was the first step to your destiny and powers, there is a science to heal. Those with that science are doctors, the healers of the world. In India, healers are second only to the Gods! In SHORTCUT 170 DOCTOR QUOTES, Dr. Bak is dedicating the 8th volume of the series to his peers, doctors, from all around the world. Doctors too, have to walk their Quest of Identity, to heal from their pain and to walk their legend. Doctors need to heal and rejuvenate to keep healing the world. If healing is their science, in SHORTCUT, they will access the power of leveraging.

SUCCESS IS A CHOICE -060
BLUEPRINTS FOR HEALTH PROFESSIONALS
BY Dr. BAK NGUYEN

In SUCCESS IS A CHOICE, FINANCIAL MILLIONAIRE BLUEPRINTS FOR HEALTH PROFESSIONALS, Dr. Bak is breaking down the strategy to success for all those wearing white coats and scrubs: doctors, dentists, pharmacists, chiropractors, nurses, etc. Success is broken down into three key strategies: Financial Leverage - Compressing time - Always being in control. Presented by MILLION DOLLAR MINDSET, the book is covering more than the ways to create wealth, but also how to reach happiness and to live a life without regrets.Dr. Bak is a successful cosmetic dentist with nearly 20 years of experience. He founded Mdex & Co, a company with the promise of reforming the whole dental industry for the better. While doing so, he discovered a passion for writing and for sharing. Multiple times World Record, Dr. Bak is writing a book every 2 weeks for the last 30 months. This is his 60th book, and he is still practicing. How he does it, is what he is sharing with us, SUCCESS, HAPPINESS, and mostly FREEDOM to all Health Professionals.

SYMPHONY OF SKILLS -001
BY Dr. BAK NGUYEN

You will enlighten the world with your potential. I can't wait to see all the differences that you will have in our world. Remember that power comes with responsibility. We can feel in his presence, a genuine force, a depth of energy, confidence, innocence, courage, and intelligence. Bak is always looking for answers, morning and night, he wants to understand the why and the why not. This book is the essence of the man. Dr. Bak is a force of nature who bears proudly his title eHappy. The man never ceases smiling nor spreading his good vibe wherever he passes. He is not trapped in the nostalgia of the past nor the satisfaction of the present, he embodies the joy of what's possible, what's to come. The more we read, the more we share, and we live. That is Bak, he charms us to evolve and to share his points of view, and before we know it, we are walking by his side, a journey we never saw coming.

T

THE 90 DAYS CHALLENGE -061
BY Dr. BAK NGUYEN

THE 90 DAYS CHALLENGE, is Dr. Bak's journey into the unknown. Overachiever writing 2 books a month on average, for the last 30 months, ambitious CEO, Industries' Disruptor, Dr. Bak seems to have success in everything he touches. Everything except the control of his weight. For nearly 20 years, he struggles with an overweight problem. Every time he scored big, he added on a little more weight. Well, this time, he exposes himself out there, in real-time and without filter, accepting the challenge of his brother-in-law, DON VO to lose 45 pounds within 90 days. That's half a pound a day, for three months. He will have to do so while keeping all of his other challenges on track, writing books at a world record pace, leading the dental industry into the new ERA, and keep seeing his patients. Undoubtedly entertaining, this is the journey of an ALPHA who simply won't give up. But this time, nothing is sure.

THE BOOK OF LEGENDS -024
BY Dr. BAK NGUYEN & WILLIAM BAK

The Book of Legends vol. 1 the story behind the world record of Dr. Bak and his son, William Bak. All Dr. Bak had in mind was to keep his promise of writing a book with his son. They ended up writing 8 children's books within a month, scoring a new world record. William is also the youngest author having published in two languages. Those are world records waiting to be confirmed. History will say: to celebrate a first world record (writing 15 books / 15 months), for the love of his son, he will have scored a second world record: to write 8 books within a month! THE BOOK OF LEGENDS vol. 1 This is both a magical journey for both a father and a son looking to connect and to find themselves. Join Dr. Bak and William Bak in their journey and their love for Life!

THE BOOK OF LEGENDS 2 -041
BY Dr. BAK NGUYEN & WILLIAM BAK

THE BOOK OF LEGENDS vol. 2 is the sequel of "CINDERELLA" but a true story between a father and his son. Together they have discovered a bond and a way to connect. The first BOOK OF LEGENDS covered the time of the first four books they wrote together within a month. The second BOOK OF LEGENDS is covering what happened after the curtains dropped, what happened after reality kicked back in. If the first volume was about a fairy tale in vacation time, the second volume is about making it last in real Life. Share their journey and their love of Life!

THE BOOK OF LEGENDS 3 -086
THE END OF THE INNOCENCE AGE
BY Dr. BAK NGUYEN & WILLIAM BAK

This is the third volume of the series, THE BOOK OF LEGENDS. If the first two happened as a breeze breaking world records on top of world records (27 books written as father and son), the 3rd volume took much more time to arrive. William has grown and writing chicken books is not enough anymore to ignite his imagination. Dr. Bak, as a good father, will try to follow William's growth and invented new games, technics and mind frames to keep engaging William's imagination and interest. From auditions to backstories, Dr. Bak bent backward to keep the adventure going. More than sharing the success and the glory, within THE BOOK OF LEGENDS volume 3, you are sharing the doubts and failure of a father and son refusing to let go… but who have now left MOMENTUM… until the winds blow once more in their favour. Welcome to the Alphas.

THE CONFESSION OF A LAZY OVERACHIEVER -089
REINVENT YOURSELF FROM ANY CRISIS
BY Dr. BAK NGUYEN

In THE CONFESSION OF A LAZY OVERACHIEVER, Dr. Bak is opening up to his new marketing officer, Jamie, fresh out of school. She is young, full of energy, and looking to chill and still to have it all. True to his character, Dr. Bak is giving Jamie some leeway to redefine Dr. Bak's brand to her demographic, the Millennials. This journey is about Dr. Bak satisfying the Millennials and answering their true questions in life. A rebel himself, his ambition to change the world started back on campus, some 25 years ago... then, life caught up with him. It took Dr. Bak 20 years to shake down the burdens of life, to spread his wings free from Conformity, and to start Overachieving. Doctor, CEO, and world record author, here is what Dr. Bak would have love to know 25 years ago as was still on campus. In a word, this is cheating your way to success and freedom. And yes, it is possible. Success, Money, Freedom, it all starts with a mindset and the awareness of Time. Welcome to the Alphas.

THE ENERGY FORMULA -053
BY Dr. BAK NGUYEN

THE ENERGY FORMULA is a book dedicated to help each individual to find the means to reach their purpose and goal in Life. Dr. Bak is a philosopher, a strategist, a business, an artist, and a dentist, how does he do all of that? He is doing so while mentoring proteges and leading the modernization of an entire industry. Until now, Momentum and Speed were the powers that he was building on and from. But those powers come from somewhere too. From a guide of our Quest of Identity, he became an ally in everyone's journey for happiness. THE ENERGY FORMULA is the book revealing step by step, the logic of building the right mindset and the way to ABUNDANCE and HAPPINESS, universally. It is not just a HOW TO book, but one that will change your life and guide you to the path of ABUNDANCE.

THE MODERN WOMAN -070
TO HAVE IT HAVE WITH NO SACRIFICE
BY Dr. BAK NGUYEN & Dr. EMILY LETRAN

In THE MODERN WOMAN: TO HAVE IT ALL WITH NO SACRIFICE, Dr. Bak joins forces with Dr. Emily Letran to empower all women to fulfill their desires, goals, and ambition. Both overachievers going against the odds, they are sharing their experience and wisdom to help all women to find confidence and support to redefine their lives. Dr. Emily Letran is a doctor in dentistry, an entrepreneur, author, and CERTIFIED HIGH-PERFORMANCE coach. For an Asian woman, she made it through the norms and the red tapes to find her voice. As she learned and grew with mentors, today she is sharing her secret with the energy that will motivate all of the female genders to stand for what they deserve. Alpha doctor, Bak is joining his voice and perspective since this is not about gender equality, but about personal empowerment and the quest of Identity of each, man and woman. Once more, Dr. Bak is bringing LEVERAGE and REASON to the new social deal between man and woman. This is not about gender, but about confidence.

THE POWER BEHIND THE ALPHA -008
BY TRANIE VO & Dr. BAK NGUYEN

It's been said by a "great man" that "We are born alone and we die alone." Both men and women proudly repeat those words as wisdom since. I apologize in advance, but what a fat LIE! That's what I learned and discovered in life since my mind and heart got liberated from the burden of scars and the ladders of society. I can have it all, not all at the same time, but I can have everything I put my mind and heart into. Actually, it is not completely true. I can have most of what I and Tranie put our minds into. Together, when we feel like one, there isn't much out of our reach. If I'm the mind, she's the heart; if I'm the Will, she's the means. Synergy is the core of our power.Tranie's aim is always Happiness. In Tranie's definition of life, there are no justifications, no excuses, no tomorrow. For Tranie, Happiness is measured by the minutes of every single day. This is why she's so strong and can heal people around her. That may also be why she doesn't need to talk much, since talking about the past or the future is, in her mind, dimming down the magic of the present, the Now. We both respect and appreciate that we are the whole balancing each other's equation of life, of love, of success. I was the plus and the minus, then I became the multiplication factor and grew into the exponential. And how is Tranie evolving in all of this? She is and always will be the balance. If anything, she is the equal sign of each equation.

THE POWER OF Dr. -066
THE MODERN TITLE OF NOBILITY
BY Dr. BAK NGUYEN, Dr. PAVEL KRASTEV AND COLLABORATORS

In THE POWER OF Dr., independent thinkers mean to exchange ideas. An idea can be very powerful if supported with a great work ethic. Work ethic, isn't that the main fabric of our white coats, scrubs, and title? In an era post-COVID where everything has been rebooted and that the healthcare industry is facing its own fate: to evolve or to be replaced, Dr. Bak and Dr. Pavel reveal the source of their power and their playbook to move forward, ahead.The power we all hold is our resilience and discipline. We put that for years at the service of our profession, from a surgical perspective. Now, we can harness that same power to rewrite the rules, the industry, and our future. Post-COVID, the rules are being rewritten, will you be part of the team or left behind?
"You can be in control!" More than personal growth and a motivational book, THE POWER OF Dr. is an awakening call to the doctor you look at when you graduate, with hope, with honour, with determination.

THE POWER OF YES -010
VOLUME ONE: IMPACT
BY Dr. BAK NGUYEN

In THE POWER OF YES, Dr. Bak is sharing his journey opening up and embracing the world, one day at a time, one ask at a time, one wish at a time. Far from a dare, saying YES allowed Dr. Bak to rewrite his mindsets and to break all the boundaries. This book is not one written a few days or weeks, but the accumulation of a journey for 12 months. The journeys started as Dr. Bak said YES to his producer to go on stage and to speak... That YES opened a world of possibilities. Dr. Bak embraced each and every one of them. 12 months later, he is celebrating the new world record of writing 9 books written over a period of 12 months. To him, it will be a miss, missing the 12 on 12 mark. To the rest of the world, they just saw the birth of a force of nature, the Alpha force. THE POWER OF YES is comprised of all the introduction of the adult books written by Dr. Bak within the first 12 months. Chapter by chapter, you can walk in his footstep seeing and smelling what he has. This is reality literature with a twist of POWER. THE POWER OF YES! Discover your potential and your power. This is the POWER OF YES, volume one. Welcome to the Alphas.

THE POWER OF YES 2 -037
VOLUME TWO: SHAPELESS
BY Dr. BAK NGUYEN

In THE POWER OF YES, volume 2, Dr. Bak is continuing his journey discovering his powers and influence. After 12 months embracing the world saying YES, he rose as an emerging force: he's been recognized as an INDUSTRIES DISRUPTOR, got nominated ERNST AND YOUNG ENTREPRENEUR OF THE YEAR, wrote 9 books within 12 months while launching the most ambitious private endeavour to reform his own industry, the dental field. Contender too many WORLD RECORDS, Dr. Bak is doing all of that in parallel. And yes, he is sleeping his nights and yes, he is writing his book himself, from the screen of his iPhone! Far from satisfied, Dr. Bak missed the mark of writing 12 books within 12 months and everything else is shaping and moving, and could come crumbling down at each turn. Now that Dr. Bak understands his powers, he is looking to test them and to push them to their limits, looking to keep scoring world records while materializing his vision and enterprises. This is the awakening of a Force of Nature looking to change the world for the better while having fun sharing. Welcome to the Alphas.

THE POWER OF YES 3 -046
VOLUME THREE: LIMITLESS
BY Dr. BAK NGUYEN

In THE POWER OF YES, volume 3, the journey of Dr. Bak continues where the last volume left, in front of 300 plus people showing up to his first solo event, a Dr. Bak's event. On stage and in this book, Dr. Bak reveals how 12 months saying YES to everything changed his life... actually, it was 18 months.
From a dentist looking to change the world from a dental chair into a multiple times world record author, the journey of openness is a rendez-vous with Fate. Dr. Bak is sharing almost in real-time his journey, experiences, but above all, his feelings, doubts, and comebacks. From one book to the next, from one journey to the next, follow the adventure of a man looking to find his name, his worth, and his place in the world. Doing so, he is touching people Doing so, he is touching people and initiating their rises. Are you ready for more? Are you ready to meet your Fate and Destiny? Welcome to the Alphas.

THE POWER OF YES 4 -087
VOLUME FOUR: PURPOSE
BY Dr. BAK NGUYEN

In THE POWER OF YES, volume 4, the journey continues days after where the last volume left. After setting the new world record of writing 48 books within 24 months, Dr. Bak is not ready to stop. As volume one covers 12 months of journey, volume 2 covers 6 months. Well, volume 3 covers 4 months. The speed is building up and increasing, steadily. This is volume 4, RISING, after breaking the sound barrier. Dr. Bak has reached a state where he is above most resistance and friction, he is now in a universe of his own, discovering his powers as he walks his journeys. This is no fiction story or wishful thinking, THE POWER OF YES is the journey of Dr. Bak, from one world record to the next, from one book to the next. You too can walk your own legend, you just need to listen to your innersole and to open up to the opportunity. May you get inspiration from the legendary journey of Dr. Bak and find your own Destiny. Welcome to the Alphas.

THE RISE OF THE UNICORN -038
BY Dr. BAK NGUYEN & Dr. JEAN DE SERRES

In THE RISE OF THE UNICORN, Dr. Bak is joining forces with his friend and mentor, Dr. Jean De Serres. Together both men had many achievements in their respective industries, but the advent of eHappyPedia, THE RISE OF THE UNICORN is a personal project dear to both of them: the QUEST OF HAPPINESS and its empowerment. This book is a special one since you are witnessing the conversation between two entrepreneurs looking to change the world by building unique tools and media. Just like any enterprise, the ride is never a smooth one in the park on a beautiful day. But this is about eHappyPedia, it is about happiness, right? So it will happen and with a smile attached to it! The unique value of this book is that you are sharing the ups and downs of the launch of a Unicorn, not just the glory of the fame, but also the doubts and challenges on the way. May it inspire you on your own journey to success and happiness.

THE RISE OF THE UNICORN 2 -076
eHappyPedia
BY Dr. BAK NGUYEN & Dr. JEAN DE SERRES

This is 2 years after starting the first tome. Dr. Bak's brand is picking up, between the accumulation of records and the recognition. eHappyPedia is now hot for a comeback. In THE RISE OF THE UNICORN 2, Dr. Bak is retracing and addressing each of Dr. Jean De Serres' concerns about the weakness of the first version of eHappyPedia and the eHappy movement. This is the sort of the creation and a UNICORN both in finance and in psychology. Never before, you will assist in such daily and decision-making process of a world phenomenon and of a company. Dr. Bak and Dr. De Serres are literally using the process of writing this series of books to plan and to brainstorm the birth of a bluechip. More than an intriguing story, this is the journey of 2 experienced entrepreneurs changing the world.

THE U.A.X STORY -072
THE ULTIMATE AUDIO EXPERIENCE
BY Dr. BAK NGUYEN

This is the story of the ULTIMATE AUDIO EXPERIENCE, U.A.X. Follow Dr. Bak's footstep on how he invented a new way to read and to learn. Dr. Bak brings his experience as a movie producer and a director to elevate the reading experience to another level with entertaining value and make it accessible to everyone, auditive, and visual people alike.

Three years plus of research and development, countless hours of trials and errors, Dr. Bak finally solved his puzzle: having written more than 1.1 million words. The irony is that he does not like to read, he likes audiobooks! U.A.X. finally allowed the opening of Dr. Bak's entire library to a new genre and media. U.A.X. is the new way to learn and enjoy Audiobooks. Made to be entertaining while keeping the self-educational value of a book, U.A.X. will appeal to both auditive and visual people. U.A.X. is the blockbuster of the Audiobooks. The format has already been approved by iTunes, Amazon, Spotify, and all major platforms for global distribution and streaming.

TIMING - TIME MANAGEMENT ON STEROIDS -074
BY Dr. BAK NGUYEN & WILLIAM BAK

In TIMING, TIME MANAGEMENT ON STEROIDS, Dr. Bak is sharing his secret to keep overachieving, overdelivering while raising the bar higher and higher. We all have 24 hours in a day, so how can some do so much more than others. Dr. Bak is not only sharing his secrets and mindset about time and efficiency, he is literally living his own words as this book is written within his last sprint to set the next world record of writing 100 books within 4 years, with only 31 days to go. With 8 books to write in 31 days, that's a little less than 4 days per book! Share the journey of a man surfing the change and looking to see where is the limit of the human mind, writing. In the meantime, understand his leverage, mindset, and secrets to challenge your own limits and dreams.

THE VACCINE -077
BY Dr. BAK NGUYEN & WILLIAM BAK

In THE VACCINE, A TALE OF SPIES AND ALIENS, Dr. Bak reprise his role as mentor to William, his 10 years-old son, both as co-author and as doctor. William is living through the COVID war and has accumulated many, many questions. That morning, they got out all at once. From a conversation between father and son, Dr. Bak is making science into words keeping the interest of his son a Saturday morning in bed. William is not just an audience, he is responsible to map the field with his questions. What started as a morning conversation between father and son, became within the next hour, a great project, their 23rd book together. Learn about the virus, vaccination while entertaining your kids.

TO OVERACHIEVE EVERYTHING BEING LAZY -090
CHEAT YOUR WAY TO SUCCESS
BY Dr. BAK NGUYEN

In TO OVERACHIEVE EVERYTHING BEING LAZY, Dr. Bak retaking his role talking to the millennials, the next generation. If in the first tome of the series LAZY, Dr. Bak addresses the general audience of millennials, especially young women, he is dedicating this tome to the ALPHA amongst the millennials, those aiming for the moon and looking, not only to be happy but to change the world. This is not another take on how to cheat your way to success or how to leverage laziness, but this is the recipe to build overachievers and rainmakers. For the young leaders with ambitions and talent, understanding TIME and ENERGY are crucial from your first steps writing your our legend. If Dr. Bak had the chance to do it all over again, this is how he would do it! Welcome to the Alphas.

TORNADO -067
FORCE OF CHANGE
BY Dr. BAK NGUYEN

In TORNADO - FORCE OF CHANGE Dr. Bak is writing solo. In the midst of the COVID war, change is not a good intention anymore. Change, constant change has become a new reality, a new norm. From somebody who holds the title of Industries' Disruptor, how does he yield change to stay in control? Well, the changes from the COVID war are constant fear and much loss of individual liberty. Some can endure the change, some will ride it. Dr. Bak is sharing his angle of navigating the changes, yielding the improvisations, and to reinvent the goals, the means to stay relevant. From fighting to keep his companies Dr. Bak went on to let go the uncontrollable to embrace the opportunity, he reinvented himself to ride the change and create opportunities from an unprecedented crisis. This is the story of a man refusing to kneel and accept defeat, smiling back at faith to find leverage and hope.

TOUCHSTONE -073
LEVERAGING TODAY'S PSYCHOLOGICAL SMOG
BY Dr. BAK NGUYEN & Dr. KEN SEROTA

TOUCHSTONE, LEVERAGING TODAY'S PSYCHOLOGICAL SMOG is mapping to navigate and to thrive in today's high and constant stress environment. After 40 years in practice, Dr. Serota is concerned about the evolution of the career of health care professionals and the never-ending level of stress. What is stress, what are its effects, damages, and symptoms? If COVID-19 revealed to the world that we are fragile, it also revealed most of the broken and the flaws of our system. For now a century, dentistry has been a champion in depression, Dr.ug addiction, and suicide rate, and the curve is far from flattening. Dr. Bak is sharing his perspective and experience dealing with stress and how to leverage it into a constructive force. From the stress of a doctor with no right to failure to the stress of an entrepreneur never knowing the future, Dr. Bak is sharing his way to use stress as leverage.

ABOUT THE AUTHORS

From Canada, **Dr BAK NGUYEN**, Nominee Ernst and Young Entrepreneur of the year, Grand Homage Lys DIVERSITY, and LinkedIn & TownHall Achiever of the year. Dr Bak is a cosmetic dentist, CEO and founder of Mdex & Co. His company is revolutionizing the dental field. Speaker and motivator, he wrote 72 books over 36 months accumulating many world records (to be officialized).

- **ENTREPRENEURSHIP**
- **LEADERSHIP**
- **QUEST OF IDENTITY**
- **DENTISTRY AND MEDICINE**
- **PARENTING**
- **CHILDREN BOOKS**
- **PHILOSOPHY**

In 2003, he founded Mdex, a dental company upon which in 2018, he launched the most ambitious private endeavour to reform the dental industry, Canada wide. Philosopher, he has close to his heart the quest of happiness of the people surrounding him, patients and colleagues alike. In 2020, he launched an International collaborative initiative named **THE ALPHAS** to share knowledge and for Entrepreneurs and Doctors to thrive through the Greatest Pandemic and Economic depression of our time.

In 2016, he co-found with Tranie Vo, Emotive World Incorporated, a tech research company to use technology to empower happiness and sharing. U.A.X. the ultimate audio experience is the landmark project on which the team is advancing, utilizing the technics of the movie industry and the advancement in ARTIFICIAL INTELLIGENCE to save the book industry and to upgrade the continuing education space.

These projects have allowed Dr Nguyen to attract interests from the international and diplomatic community and he is now the center of a global discussion in the wellbeing and the future of the health profession. It is in that matter that he shares his thoughts and encourages the health community to share their own stories.

"It's not worth it go through it alone! Together, we stand, alone, we fall."

Motivational speaker and serial entrepreneur, philosopher and author, from his own words, Dr Nguyen describes himself as a dentist by circumstances, an entrepreneur by nature and a communicator by passion.

He also holds recognitions from the Canadian Parliament and the Canadian Senate.

www.DrBakNguyen.com

AMAZON - BARNES & NOBLE - APPLE BOOKS - KINDLE
SPOTIFY - APPLE MUSIC

ULTIMATE AUDIO EXPERIENCE

A new way to learn and enjoy Audiobooks. Made to be entertaining while keeping the self-educational value of a book, UAX will appeal to both auditive and visual people. UAX is the blockbuster of the Audiobooks.

UAX will cover most of Dr Bak's books, and is now negotiating to bring more authors and more titles to the UAX concept. Now streaming on Spotify, Apple Music and available for download on all major music platforms. Give it a try today!

AMAZON - BARNES & NOBLE - APPLE BOOKS - KINDLE
SPOTIFY - APPLE MUSIC

FROM THE SAME AUTHOR
Dr. Bak Nguyen

TITLES AVAILABLE AT

www.DrBakNguyen.com

MAJOR LEAGUES' ACCESS

FACTEUR HUMAIN -035
LE LEADERSHIP DU SUCCÈS
par Dr. BAK NGUYEN & CHRISTIAN TRUDEAU

THE RISE OF THE UNICORN -038
BY Dr. BAK NGUYEN & Dr. JEAN DE SERRES

CHAMPION MINDSET -039
LEARNING TO WIN
BY Dr. BAK NGUYEN & CHRISTOPHE MULUMBA

THE RISE OF THE UNICORN 2 -076
eHappyPedia
BY Dr. BAK NGUYEN & Dr. JEAN DE SERRES

BRANDING -044
BALANCING STRATEGY AND EMOTIONS
BY Dr. BAK NGUYEN

002 - **La Symphonie des Sens**
ENTREPREUNARIAT
par Dr. BAK NGUYEN

006 - **INDUSTRIES DISRUPTORS**
BY Dr. BAK NGUYEN

007 - **Changing the World from a dental chair**
BY Dr. BAK NGUYEN

008 - **The Power Behind the Alpha**
BY TRANIE VO & Dr. BAK NGUYEN

036 - **SELFMADE**
GRATITUDE AND HUMILITY
BY Dr. BAK NGUYEN

072 - **THE U.A.X. STORY**
THE ULTIMATE AUDIO EXPERIENCE
BY Dr. BAK NGUYEN

088 - **CRYPTOCONOMICS 101**
MY PERSONAL JOURNEY
FROM 50K TO 1 MILLION
BY Dr BAK NGUYEN

BUSINESS

SYMPHONY OF SKILLS -001
BY Dr. BAK NGUYEN

CHILDREN'S BOOK
with William Bak

The Trilogy of Legends

THE LEGEND OF THE CHICKEN HEART -016
LA LÉGENDE DU COEUR DE POULET -017
BY Dr. BAK NGUYEN & WILLIAM BAK

THE LEGEND OF THE LION HEART -018
LA LÉGENDE DU COEUR DE LION -019
BY Dr. BAK NGUYEN & WILLIAM BAK

THE LEGEND OF THE DRAGON HEART -020
LA LÉGENDE DU COEUR DE DRAGON -021
BY Dr. BAK NGUYEN & WILLIAM BAK

WE ARE ALL DRAGONS -022
NOUS TOUS, DRAGONS -023
BY Dr. BAK NGUYEN & WILLIAM BAK

The Collection of the Chicken

THE 9 SECRETS OF THE SMART CHICKEN -025
LES 9 SECRETS DU POULET INTELLIGENT -026
BY Dr. BAK NGUYEN & WILLIAM BAK

THE SECRET OF THE FAST CHICKEN -027
LE SECRETS DU POULET RAPIDE -028
BY Dr. BAK NGUYEN & WILLIAM BAK

THE LEGEND OF THE SUPER CHICKEN -029
LA LÉGENDE DU SUPER POULET -030
BY Dr. BAK NGUYEN & WILLIAM BAK

031- **THE STORY OF THE CHICKEN SHIT**
032- **L'HISTOIRE DU CACA DE POULET**
BY Dr. BAK NGUYEN & WILLIAM BAK

033- **WHY CHICKEN CAN'T DREAM?**
034- **POURQUOI LES POULETS NE RÊVENT PAS?**
BY Dr. BAK NGUYEN & WILLIAM BAK

057- **THE STORY OF THE CHICKEN NUGGET**
083- **HISTOIRE DE POULET: LA PÉPITE**
BY Dr. BAK NGUYEN & WILLIAM BAK

082- **CHICKEN FOREVER**
084- **POULET POUR TOUJOURS**
BY Dr BAK NGUYEN & WILLIAM BAK

THE SPIES AND ALIENS COLLECTION

077- **THE VACCINE**
079- **LE VACCIN**
077B- **LA VACUNA**
BY Dr BAK NGUYEN & WILLIAM BAK
TRANSLATION BY BRENDA GARCIA

DENTISTRY

PROFESSION HEALTH - TOME ONE -005
THE UNCONVENTIONAL
QUEST OF HAPPINESS
BY Dr. BAK NGUYEN, Dr. MIRJANA SINDOLIC,
Dr. ROBERT DURAND AND COLLABORATORS

HOW TO NOT FAIL AS A DENTIST -047
BY Dr. BAK NGUYEN

SUCCESS IS A CHOICE -060
BLUEPRINTS FOR HEALTH
PROFESSIONALS
BY Dr. BAK NGUYEN

RELEVANCY - TOME TWO -064
REINVENTING OURSELVES TO SURVIVE
BY Dr. BAK NGUYEN & Dr. PAUL OUELLETTE AND
COLLABORATORS

MIDAS TOUCH -065
POST-COVID DENTISTRY
BY Dr. BAK NGUYEN, Dr. JULIO REYNAFARJE AND
Dr. PAUL OUELLETTE

THE POWER OF DR -066
THE MODERN TITLE OF NOBILITY
BY Dr. BAK NGUYEN, Dr. PAVEL KRASTEV AND
COLLABORATORS

QUEST OF IDENTITY

004- **IDENTITY**
THE ANTHOLOGY OF QUESTS
BY Dr. BAK NGUYEN

011- **HYBRID**
THE MODERN QUEST OF IDENTITY
BY Dr. BAK NGUYEN

LIFESTYLE

045- **HORIZON, BUILDING UP THE VISION**
VOLUME ONE
BY Dr. BAK NGUYEN

048- **HORIZON, ON THE FOOTSTEPS OF TITANS**
VOLUME TWO
BY Dr. BAK NGUYEN

068- **HORIZON, DREAMING OF TRAVELING**
VOLUME THREE
BY Dr. BAK NGUYEN

MILLION DOLLAR MINDSET

MOMENTUM TRANSFER -009
BY Dr. BAK NGUYEN & Coach DINO MASSON

LEVERAGE -014
COMMUNICATION INTO SUCCESS
BY Dr. BAK NGUYEN AND COLLABORATORS

HOW TO WRITE A BOOK IN 30 DAYS -042
BY Dr. BAK NGUYEN

POWER -043
EMOTIONAL INTELLIGENCE
BY Dr. BAK NGUYEN

HOW TO WRITE A SUCCESSFUL BUSINESS PLAN -049
BY Dr BAK NGUYEN & ROUBA SAKR

MINDSET ARMORY -050
BY Dr. BAK NGUYEN

MASTERMIND, 7 WAYS INTO THE BIG LEAGUE -052
BY Dr. BAK NGUYEN & JONAS DIOP

PLAYBOOK INTRODUCTION -055
BY Dr. BAK NGUYEN

PLAYBOOK INTRODUCTION 2 -056
BY Dr. BAK NGUYEN

062- **RISING**
TO WIN MORE THAN YOU ARE AFRAID TO LOSE
BY Dr. BAK NGUYEN

067- **TORNADO**
FORCE OF CHANGE
BY Dr. BAK NGUYEN

071- **BOOTCAMP**
BOOKS TO REWRITE MINDSETS INTO WINNING STATES OF MIND
BY Dr. BAK NGUYEN

078- **POWERPLAY**
HOW TO BUILD THE PERFECT TEAM
BY Dr. BAK NGUYEN

074- **TIMING**
TIME MANAGEMENT ON STEROIDS
BY Dr. BAK NGUYEN

PARENTING

024- **THE BOOK OF LEGENDS**
BY Dr. BAK NGUYEN & WILLIAM BAK

041- **THE BOOK OF LEGENDS 2**
BY Dr. BAK NGUYEN & WILLIAM BAK

086- **THE BOOK OF LEGENDS 3**
THE END OF THE INNOCENCE AGE
BY Dr. BAK NGUYEN & WILLIAM BAK

PERSONAL GROWTH

REBOOT -012
MIDLIFE CRISIS
BY Dr. BAK NGUYEN

HUMILITY FOR SUCCESS -051
BALANCING STRATEGY AND EMOTIONS
BY Dr. BAK NGUYEN

THE ENERGY FORMULA -053
BY Dr. BAK NGUYEN

AMONGST THE ALPHA -058
BY Dr. BAK NGUYEN & COACH JONAS DIOP

AMONGST THE ALPHA vol.2 -059
ON THE OTHER SIDE
BY Dr. BAK NGUYEN & COACH JONAS DIOP

THE 90 DAYS CHALLENGE -061
BY Dr. BAK NGUYEN

EMPOWERMENT -069
BY Dr BAK NGUYEN

THE MODERN WOMAN -070
TO HAVE IT HAVE WITH NO SACRIFICE
BY Dr. BAK NGUYEN & Dr. EMILY LETRAN

ALPHA LADDERS -075
CAPTAIN OF YOUR DESTINY
BY Dr BAK NGUYEN & JONAS DIOP

080- **1SELF**
REINVENT YOURSELF
FROM ANY CRISIS
BY Dr BAK NGUYEN

THE LAZY FRANCHISE

089- **THE CONFESSION OF
A LAZY OVERACHIEVER**
BY Dr BAK NGUYEN

090- **TO OVERACHIEVE
EVERYTHING BEING LAZY**
CHEAT YOUR WAY TO SUCCESS
BY Dr BAK NGUYEN

PHILOSOPHY

003- **LEADERSHIP** -003
PANDORA'S BOX
BY Dr. BAK NGUYEN

015- **FORCES OF NATURE**
FORGING THE CHARACTER
OF WINNERS
BY Dr BAK NGUYEN

040- **KRYPTO**
TO SAVE THE WORLD
BY Dr. BAK NGUYEN & ILYAS BAKOUCH

ALPHA LADDERS 2 -081
SHAPING LEADERS AND ACHIEVERS
BY Dr BAK NGUYEN & BRENDA GARCIA

MIRROR -085
BY Dr BAK NGUYEN

099- **306 HAPPINESS QUOTES**
SHORTCUT VOLUME SEVEN
BY Dr. BAK NGUYEN

100 - **170 DOCTOR QUOTES**
SHORTCUT VOLUME EIGHT
BY Dr. BAK NGUYEN

SHORTCUT

SOCIETY

408 HEALING QUOTES -093
SHORTCUT VOLUME ONE
BY Dr. BAK NGUYEN

408 GROWTH QUOTES -094
SHORTCUT VOLUME TWO
BY Dr. BAK NGUYEN

365 LEADERSHIP QUOTES -095
SHORTCUT VOLUME THREE
BY Dr. BAK NGUYEN

518 CONFIDENCE QUOTES -096
SHORTCUT VOLUME FOUR
BY Dr. BAK NGUYEN

317 SUCCESS QUOTES -097
SHORTCUT VOLUME FIVE
BY Dr. BAK NGUYEN

376 POWER QUOTES -098
SHORTCUT VOLUME SIX
BY Dr. BAK NGUYEN

013 - **LE RÊVE CANADIEN**
D'IMMIGRANT À MILLIONNAIRE
par DR BAK NGUYEN

054 - **CHOC**
LE JARDIN D'EDITH
par DR BAK NGUYEN

063 - **AFTERMATH**
BUSINESS AFTER THE GREAT PAUSE
BY Dr BAK NGUYEN & Dr ERIC LACOSTE

073 - **TOUCHSTONE**
LEVERAGING TODAY'S
PSYCHOLOGICAL SMOG
BY Dr BAK NGUYEN & Dr KEN SEROTA

TO COME - **COVIDCONOMICS**
THE GENERATION AHEAD
BY Dr BAK NGUYEN

THE POWER OF YES

THE POWER OF YES - 010
VOLUME ONE: IMPACT
BY Dr BAK NGUYEN

THE POWER OF YES 2 - 037
VOLUME TWO: SHAPELESS
BY Dr BAK NGUYEN

046 - **THE POWER OF YES 3**
VOLUME THREE: LIMITLESS
BY Dr BAK NGUYEN

087 - **THE POWER OF YES 4**
VOLUME FOUR: PURPOSE
BY Dr BAK NGUYEN

091 - **THE POWER OF YES 5**
VOLUME FIVE: ALPHA
BY Dr BAK NGUYEN

092 - **THE POWER OF YES 6**
VOLUME SIX: PERSPECTIVE
BY Dr BAK NGUYEN

TITLES AVAILABLE AT
www.DrBakNguyen.com

AMAZON - BARNES & NOBLE - APPLE BOOKS - KINDLE
SPOTIFY - APPLE MUSIC